Praise for *Between the Covers*

'What better gift to give f~~~~ C~~~~~~~~
wonderfully i~~~~~~~~~~~~~
Jilly Coop~~~

'No one else can m~~~~~~~~~~~~~~~y, sometimes
at the same time, quite like Jilly Cooper'
Gill Sims

'Jilly Cooper's non-fiction is just as
entertaining as her novels'
Pandora Sykes

'This book has given me so much pleasure'
Alan Titchmarsh

'Britain needs this jolly Jilly Cooper collection . . . Line after
line, anecdote after anecdote is laugh-out-loud funny,
the prose bouncing along like a labrador puppy'
The Times

'There are so many lifestyle columnists today, you forget
that Cooper did it first and did it best'
The Telegraph

'A collection of Jilly Cooper's vintage newspaper columns
is bitchy, sexy, insightful and, most of all, great fun'
Observer

'She is simply a legend'
Daily Mail

Jilly Cooper is a journalist, author and media superstar. The author of many number one bestselling novels, she lives in Gloucestershire.

She has been awarded honorary doctorates by the Universities of Gloucestershire and Anglia Ruskin, and won the inaugural Comedy Women in Print lifetime achievement award in 2019. She was appointed CBE in 2018 for services to literature and charity.

Also by Jilly Cooper

For more information on Jilly Cooper and her books, please visit
www.jillycooper.co.uk or www.facebook.com/JillyCooperOfficial

Between the Covers

sex, socialising and survival

Jilly Cooper

CORGI BOOKS

TRANSWORLD PUBLISHERS
Penguin Random House, One Embassy Gardens,
8 Viaduct Gardens, London SW11 7BW
www.penguin.co.uk

Transworld is part of the Penguin Random House group of companies
whose addresses can be found at global.penguinrandomhouse.com

First published in Great Britain in 2020 by Bantam Press
an imprint of Transworld Publishers
Corgi edition published 2021

A CIP catalogue record for this book is available from the British Library.

ISBN
9780552178082

Typeset in Adobe Garamond Pro by Integra Software Services Pvt. Ltd, Pondicherry.

Printed and bound in Great Britain by Clays Ltd, Elcograf S.p.A.

The authorized representative in the EEA is Penguin Random House Ireland,
Morrison Chambers, 32 Nassau Street, Dublin D02 YH68.

Penguin Random House is committed to a sustainable
future for our business, our readers and our planet. This book
is made from Forest Stewardship Council® certified paper.

To the late Godfrey Smith

With love and gratitude

CONTENTS

AUTHOR'S NOTE

Nineteen sixty-eight was a miracle year for me. At thirty-one, I was poised to give up my job in publishing, because my husband Leo and I were about to adopt a longed-for baby boy.

Then, at a dinner party, I sat next to the glorious Godfrey Smith, ex-president of the Oxford Union, great journalist, author of many fine books, one of which, *The Business of Loving*, was a Book Society Choice. Godfrey was also editor of the *Sunday Times* colour magazine. During dinner I regaled him with tales of how disastrous I was domestically as a young working wife. I cited one occasion when my red silk scarf strayed into a launderette wash, so my husband Leo's rugger kit came out streaked like the dawn, and he boasted of being the only member of the rugger team with a rose-pink jockstrap.

Godfrey laughed a great deal and asked me to write a piece about it, which he published in the colour mag in early 1969.

This was enhanced by a very flattering photograph of me joyfully holding our new baby, Felix.

Imagine my excitement when a week later Harold Evans, the great overall editor of the *Sunday Times*, summoned me and offered me my own column to write about anything I liked. The column amazingly lasted for thirteen years through the seventies and early eighties, often chronicling my chaos as a wife and mother working from home, and our lunatic but hugely enjoyable social life.

Sunday Times readers did tend to like or loathe what I wrote, with my first column upsetting them so much, Harold Evans was able to fill my next week's column with their furious letters.

I am therefore delighted that my dear publishers Transworld are reissuing a collection of some of my favourite columns. You will find the selection covers among other things our London life in the sexy sixties and seventies and our move from Fulham to Putney Common.

What I love most about the book is that it brings back, not only my macho, forthright, funny husband Leo, who died of Parkinson's disease in 2013, but also my children Felix and Emily as they were growing up, my sweet parents and so many friends and adventures.

On the other hand, rereading the pieces, some fifty years later, I wonder: *Was this really me, so up myself and so utterly obsessed with sex? Did I really dare write that?* But I do so hope that readers both young and old enjoy them.

Lots of love,
Jilly Cooper CBE xx

The Young Wife's Tale

Looking back on the first fraught year of my marriage, I realise we lived in total screaming chaos. I spent most of my time in tears – not tears of misery, but exhaustion. I couldn't cook, I couldn't sew, I had no idea about running a house, my knowledge of sex was limited to Eustace Chesser and Lady Chatterley – yet suddenly I was on trial: sexually, domestically, commercially, socially, and aware that I was inadequate on every count.

My husband's remarks, like: 'Do you really think the book case is the right place for a mouldy apple?' would wound me to the quick – or that despairing 'Let's start as we mean to go on' as he looked at the flotsam of clothes strewn over the bedroom, and resented the fact that I had already appropriated five and three-quarters of the six drawers and three out of four of the coat hangers.

As we made love most of the night, I found it impossible to get up in the morning, cook breakfast, do my face and get out of the house by 8.15. Then followed an exhausting day at the office, only punctuated by one of those scurrying, shopping lunches. I was seldom home – due to the caprice of London Transport – before seven o'clock. Then there was the bed to be made, breakfast to be washed up, the cat to be fed and chatted up, the day to be discussed and supper to be cooked. This was a proper supper (garlic, aubergines and all). The way to a man's heart was supposed to be through his stomach, so there was no getting away with pork pie or scrambled eggs. When I cooked moussaka for the first time we didn't eat until one o'clock in the morning.

We were very gregarious and were asked out a great deal. My husband also played cricket and rugger at weekends, so as a besotted newly-wed I was only too happy to abandon the housework and watch him score tries and centuries.

As a result the flat became dirtier and more chaotic. The only time we ever really cleaned it up was when in-laws or relations came to stay, and my husband would then say that it was just like a barracks before the annual general inspection. 'How pretty those dead flowers look,' said a kindly aunt. 'Have they become fashionable in London?'

The only other possible moment to clean the flat was on my husband's occasional TA nights. Then I would hare round like a maniac, dusting and polishing; hoping, for once, to welcome him home scented and beautiful in a negligée with a faint smell of onions drifting from the kitchen. It never worked. Invariably he would let himself in unnoticed to find me tackling a mountain of dust under the bed with my bottom sticking out.

It was only after nine months, when the ice compartment wouldn't shut, that I learnt for the first time about defrosting the fridge. Things in the fridge were another headache. There were always those nine reproachful bowls of dripping, the tins of blackening tomato purée, the fish stock that never graduated into soup and the lettuce liquidising in the vegetable compartment.

Laundry was another nightmare. It took me months to master the mysteries of the launderette. Very early on in our marriage, a red silk scarf found its way into the machine with the rest of the washing. My husband's seven shirts came out streaked crimson like the dawn, and for days he wore cyclamen underpants and claimed he was the only member of the fifteen with a rose-pink jock-strap. Once the washing was done it lay around in pillowcases for ages, waiting to be ironed. My mother-in-law once slept peacefully and unknowingly on a pillowcase full of wet clothes.

In fact my ironing was so disastrous that for a while we tried the laundry. This presented insuperable problems. One week we were too poor to get it out, the next weekend we'd be away, the next they'd shut by the time we got there, then finally we found they'd lost all our sheets. One laundry, we discovered afterwards from the butcher next door, was notorious for 'losing' sheets.

Our own dinner parties were not without incident. The first time my mother came to dinner the blanquette of veal was flavoured with Vim, and the chocolate mousse, left in the fridge all night, was impregnated with garlic and Kit-e-Kat. The cat once ate his way through two large packets of frozen scampi and, the night my husband's boss came to dinner, stripped the salad niçoise of its tuna fish and anchovies.

The flat, as I have said, got grimier and grimier, and the same week that a fungus began to grow under the sink I overheard someone say at a cocktail party that we lived in 'engaging squalor'. It was the last straw, and we hired a daily woman. It was not a success. I spent far more time than before cleaning up before she came, and after the first few weeks the standard went down. Then my husband came back one lunch hour and found her in our bed with the electric blanket and the wireless on.

The cats – we soon acquired a second – did not add to the ease of our married life. Whenever the doorbell rang I used to drench myself in scent to cover the smell of tomcat, and in summer there were fleas. The landlord forbade pets in the house, so the day he came to look over the flat the cats were locked in the wardrobe.

In spite of the 'engaging squalor', our spare room was permanently occupied; girls who had left their lovers or husbands who had left their wives, people who came from abroad or up from the country, all found a flea-bitten home there. The hall was always full of carrier bags full of knickers or the cornucopian suitcases of birds of passage. One man came for two days and stayed for four months. One drunken Irishman who started rampaging lustfully round the flat in the still watches of the night was locked in his bedroom. Next morning we found him in the kitchen making coffee, and the imprint of his huge sleeping body remained outside on the long grass we called our lawn.

'When I was first married,' said a friend wistfully, 'I could never make mayonnaise. Humphrey kept kissing me and the oil would go in great dollops instead of drips, and the whole thing curdled. Now we've been married five years and can afford a mixer, and I make perfect mayonnaise every time now – it's my marriage that has curdled.'

We have been married seven years now – I still can't make mayonnaise – but we're not itching, and our marriage hasn't curdled. Even so I asked my husband to name, after seven years, the things that irritated him most about me.

His answers came out pat and immediate: using his razor on my legs and not washing it out; not putting tops back on tonic or soda water, or the ice tray back in the fridge; those little balls of Kleenex everywhere; the eighteen odd socks in his top drawer; the red rings of indelible lipstick on his hand-kerchief; running out of loo paper/soap/toothpaste; forgetting to turn off lights/fires/the oven; and, of course, my friends.

'OK, OK,' I said crossly. Then I remembered a poem by an American poet called John Frederick Nims, which my hus-band had sent me when I was feeling suicidal early on in our marriage, which had suddenly made everything all right:

> *My clumsiest dear, whose hands shipwreck vases,*
> *At whose quick touch all glasses chip and ring . . .*
> *Forgetting your coffee spreading on our flannel,*
> *Your lipstick grinning on our coat.*
> *So gaily in love's unbreakable heaven*

Our souls on glory of spilt Bourbon float.
Be with me, darling, early or late, smash glasses,
I will study wry music for your sake.
For should your hands drop white and empty
All the toys of the world would break.

Losing Face

I was sitting in the car with a teenage friend the other day, when a girl in a green shift and long blonde hair sauntered by.

'She's pretty,' I said, thinking narcissistically that she looked faintly like me.

'If you like that sort of thing,' said my teenage friend, shifting her chewing gum to the other side of her mouth.

'What sort of thing?' I demanded.

'Oh, those draggy clothes and that old-hat make-up. I mean, no one looks like that any more.'

I digested this and craned my neck to look in the driving mirror. Was I out of date, too? Did no one look like me either? I picked up the evening paper when I got home and found a feature on eye make-up. 'This is the face of 1971,' said the headline. 'Lashings of false eyelashes but chuck out that eyeliner.'

Charming, thought I. Eyeliner is the only thing that transforms my eyes from very piggy to not so piggy, and the only time I wore false eyelashes one of them fell off during dinner, and my host stamped on it, thinking it was an insect.

After a night of brooding, I rose early and took a bus to the West End. In one of the big department store windows were large notices announcing: 'Monsieur Claude Duval, the expert international beautician, is over for a week from France to give free advice on make-up and introduce his new range of cosmetics.' That's my boy, I thought.

M. Claude turned out to be a miracle of rare device in lilac suiting, with fixed velvety eyes, white hands that drooped like snowdrops and a rose-petal complexion. A crowd of women shoppers, resting their swelling ankles, were watching him at work.

'Remove Madame's make-up,' he told a minion as I settled into the dentist's chair. When all traces of the face of 1960 had been removed, he peered at me through a magnifying glass and gave a deep sigh – the sort of sigh that Hercules might have given when first confronted with the Augean stables.

'Madame's skin has been totally neglected,' he said.

Starting to weed my eyebrows ferociously with a pair of scissors, he regaled his enraptured audience with a list of my imperfections.

There were red veins, open pores, whiteheads. Madame also had a combination skin, and to deal with both oily patches and ultra-dry patches she would need entirely different kinds of cleansing cream, moisturisers, toning lotion, skin food, night cream, morning cream, etc.

The minions bustled round, assembling bottles on the counter. Madame, M. Claude went on, would also need anti-wrinkle cream for beneath her eyes, and soothing lotion for puffy eyelids. Madame had problem hair, too, greasy with a trace of dandruff. She must have medicated lotion.

There were now enough bottles on the counter to open a chemist's shop. Was it necessary to buy all of them? I asked nervously. M. Claude was horrified. What was the point of his giving me free advice, if I didn't buy any of his products? My skin was in a very serious condition. Did I want to look like an old woman by the time I was thirty-five?

'It is very difficult,' he told his audience with a sigh, 'to paint over an imperfect surface.' He started painting huge circles round my eyes, dark blue, now yellow – 'to reflect the yellow in Madame's eyes' – now pink, now white.

Why hadn't he perfected a lacquer that would spray an expression of permanent amiability on to the face?

I suggested. He didn't like that. 'Close the mouth,' he interrupted sourly, starting to paint my lips.

Finally, after my 'ruddy' complexion had been toned down with a thick layer of green face powder, I was allowed to look at myself in the glass. At last, the face of 1971! I gave a wail of dismay. With my rouged cheeks, carmine lips and rainbow-coloured eyes, I looked like an old tart who'd been in a punch-up.

'Wonderfully soft effect,' chorused the minions, totting up my purchases. They came to £18.50.* As I gasped with horror at the cost, M. Claude muscled in. Bearing in mind the condition of Madame's skin, he said, she had spent ridiculously little.

Oh hell, I thought, it's the end of the month. I could pay by cheque, said one of the minions, if I had identification.

I produced my passport, which she studied for a minute. 'It doesn't look like Madame,' she said suspiciously.

It wasn't. In my haste to sneak out of the house, I'd mistakenly picked up an old passport belonging to my husband's first wife. So they had to make do with a crumpled reminder from the Gas Board.

---

* £18.50 would be £263.22 today!

I staggered home with my carrier bag, waiting for a chorus of approving wolf-whistles. They didn't come. One woman I know quite well cut me dead in the street. This is the face of 1971, I told myself firmly, it'll take some getting used to.

My husband didn't recognise me when he came to the door. He assumed that expression of bright insincerity with which he greets demands for jumble or complaints about rubbish being thrown over the wall. But, slowly, an expression of horror spread over his face. 'My God, it can't be,' he said. 'What have they done to you? Will it come off?'

My teenage friend came into the hall. 'You look like a dress rehearsal for the end of the world,' she said.

'It's the face of 1971,' I faltered.

'Well, roll on 1972,' said my husband.

Disastrous Dinners

I am not one of Nature's hostesses. Even though I start cooking and bulling up the house weeks before a dinner party, I am always beset by terrible disasters.

To begin with, you can never tell if your guests are going to get on. With the loveliest people, it can be instant hackles, and that conversation-killing 'Actually I don't agree', with the steely glint in the eye.

Sometimes they don't talk at all, and in a desperate attempt to spark off chatter, I make more and more fatuous remarks. Or almost worse, the two couples get on so well that my husband and I wonder if anyone would notice if we went to bed.

A great mistake is to crack up one lot of guests to the other. 'You're going to simply adore Gideon and Samantha!' They never do.

Guests to be avoided include:

The slow eater, who insists on telling long stories and finishing up all his food.

The non-eater, who pushes her food to the side of her plate after one mouthful and then blows cigar smoke over everyone.

The wife who rings up at the last moment, and says, 'Charles is hung over and won't come, may I bring my sister, it won't foul up your numbers, will it?'

The couple who go to cocktail parties and arrive very drunk an hour and a half late when you've asked an ultra-respectable couple to meet them – then have a row, tell blue stories and fall asleep after dinner.

The bachelors who specially ask you to fix them up with a divine girl, and when you do, spend the entire evening chatting up all the married women.

The lovers who start patting each other's thighs at 9.30, whose eyes combine and turn soft at 9.40, and who are out of the house by 9.45.

The women your husband fancies. The only solution is to give them asparagus or sweetcorn – no one looks sexy with butter running down her chin.

Our house is so difficult to find that people always arrive late, which means that by the time we go into dinner, I've had so many dry Martinis I'm practically under the piano, and it no longer seems to matter that I haven't put the pota-toes on.

I get far too happy to remember where people are sup-posed to sit, so the guest of honour ends up with a kitchen knife and the side plate with rabbits round the edge that was meant for my husband.

Even if I stay sober, there are disasters. I forget about napkins and have to rush upstairs, yank them out of the laundry basket and then iron them on the floor. Or the baby decides to stub his banana out all over the carpet, as the doorbell goes.

Or the casserole turns over as I'm taking it out of the oven. Or the top of the pepper mill comes off and a shower of peppercorns cascades irretrievably into the goulash. Or the meat's tough, and I see everyone's jaws working desperately like cows chewing the cud. Or my husband starts offering everyone second helpings when there aren't any.

I forget, too, what I gave the same guests last time. 'Isn't Jilly's *pâté* heaven?' they say. 'Yes, every time I mean to ask her how she makes it.'

Once, when we were first married, we served what the butcher described as Manchurian partridges. They went so hard that every time we tried to carve them they shot across the room, like Hunca Munca's doll's-house food, and were finally even rejected by the cats.

Dining out I adore, but we do get ourselves into some terrible muddles. Time and again we've overeaten our way through a whole shepherd's pie and the remains of Sunday's rhubarb crumble, and are just loosening our belts when the telephone goes and an irate voice says: 'Aren't you coming?'

I can't say, like Maurice Bowra, that we're more dined against than dining, but I remember in the days when Robert Carrier was writing in the colour supplement we would often have last Sunday's *coq au vin* five days running in a variety of houses.

One of our dreads are those houses where we don't get enough to drink:

'We've become awfully fond of cider,' they say, pouring into eggcup-sized glasses, when my tongue is hanging out for a stiff gin. One soak I know, to guard against such circumstances, has deliberately established a reputation for incontinency so he can charge out of the room every quarter of an hour and have a swig of whisky from the flask in his coat pocket.

And then there are those terrifying grand dinners, when six people sit down at a table big enough for twenty, and one's platitudes have to carry across eight feet of polished mahogany.

I remember, too, when I was much younger, going to dinner with a very arrogant old lady who made me so nervous that, as soon as I sat down, I leapt to my feet, saying: 'I hope I haven't taken your chair.'

'These are *all* my chairs,' she said icily.

Favourite Fantasies

Whenever life becomes too boring or unpleasant, I retreat into a world of make-believe, where my *alter ego* – who is at least a stone lighter than I am – carries on a vainglorious life quite unrelated to my real existence.

I am not too happy about this 'me' of my fantasies. I watch her sometimes, slinking out of the house at dawn clad only in a mink coat, her hair dyed some exotic colour, and roaring off to Hyde Park in her Ferrari, where two American publishers are fighting a duel over her next book, then on to breakfast at the Connaught with the victor, followed by a morning's shopping at Asprey's, and lunch at the Ritz with Yves Montand. The afternoon I draw a veil over, but seven o'clock sees her off to the Bahamas for the weekend with eight pigskin suitcases.

Fantasising began when I was a child. I used to daydream continually about rescuing my nanny and my teddy-bear from a blazing house, while I myself perished in the flames and everyone, including a slightly singed bear, sobbed themselves silly at my funeral.

As I grew older, I imagined myself performing similar feats of daring but now dressed as a boy. In turn I was Dick Barton, d'Artagnan and for at least a year Nelson's cabin boy defeating the French fleet single-handed – my sex only being discovered when a cannonball shattered my thigh, whereupon Nelson would exclaim: 'Gad sir, it's a gel, and a demned brave one at that,' as I lay dying in his arms.

Later I switched to horses. Every car or train journey was whiled away jumping walls, hedges and houses as they flashed by. I read *National Velvet* and *The Maltese Cat*, and dreamed of winning the National and polo matches with a broken collarbone. Then I went away to school, and my favourite fantasy became riding home from a show, my pony garlanded with red rosettes like Poppy Day, and suddenly finding my form mistress sitting in a puddle with a broken ankle. I would heave her on to my pony and bear her home to tea, whereupon she would clasp me warmly by the hand and say gruffly: 'You're not such a clot after all.'

I was also preoccupied with being famous. Not being a great washer, I thought about becoming a Rank starlet, and every time I thumped out the 'Merry Peasant' I saw myself as Eileen Joyce, playing Grieg at the Albert Hall, changing my dress between movements. I would glide on to the platform to clamorous applause – white shoulders gleaming out of clouds of net, a cigarette holder in one hand, and in the other a long umbrella, which to me in those days epitomised chic.

When I was twelve I started dreaming about men. I became a wanton, tempestuous beauty tamed and reduced to swooning submission by one gangster after another. Members of the Mafia, Henri of Guise, a long scar running down his handsome face, Slim Callaghan, Kirk Douglas in an eye patch, sundry Goths and Visigoths; all took turns to knock me into shape.

Even allowing for poetic licentiousness, I am not proud of my fantasy self – I never dreamed of a life serving others, of being a nurse or a nun in the Congo, and I quite ruthlessly exterminated my dear parents. Heroines in fantasies never have parents – they are defenceless orphans or, in my case, alone and palely loitering with intent.

About the age of fourteen I discovered Georgette Heyer and tennis players. I went to Wimbledon for the first time and those bronzed, beautiful, stupid men affected me like a fever. I now saw myself as the laughing rebellious ward of a US tennis champion called Seixas, who had hard watchful eyes and a reputation for bad temper. Gardnar Mulloy, Budge Patty and Frank Sedgman were all fighting for my hand, but I only cared for my wicked guardian, who in turn only realised he couldn't live without me when I fainted after winning the Singles, Doubles *and* the Plate.

All these fantasies were very innocent. My heroes raised quizzical eyebrows but never anything else. They would kiss me passionately, as rockets exploded in my head. Then a row of asterisks would follow until Stage Two; when, tears streaming down his face, Kirk Douglas or the Duc de Guise would be holding my hands, as I smiled weakly up at him after producing the heir he had so long desired.

Eventually I left school, and real men took over – after my dream heroes, they were a bit of an anti-climax, particularly the first time I was kissed. No rockets, no stars, not even asterisks. The odd thing, too, is that in real life the men I like are merry, sensitive, sensual extroverts, quite unlike the haughty, cruel, humourless introverts of my dreams.

I don't think men fantasise nearly as much as women. My husband says he occasionally dreams of making a hundred before lunch for Yorkshire at Headingley, or the stands rising at Twickenham when he scores the vital try. When he was younger he imagined himself driving off in a sports car with a lush blonde, saying: "Bye, Ted, 'Bye, Christopher, 'Bye, Paul, see you!' to his smart cricketer friends.

People are always telling me I ought to daydream less and face up to the real world. But unless fantasies are used as a complete substitute for action, I can't see much harm in them. We all need the pipe dream of writing the great novel, or winning the pools, or becoming managing director and kicking all our colleagues in the teeth. The world is deep and dark and full of tigers, and we need those shimmering white castles in the air to creep into when life gets unbearable.

As Donne says: 'If I dream I have you, I have you.' But, frankly, I don't need to fantasise much these days, I lead such a full life. I've just finished washing up a tea party for all my son's little friends from Buckingham Palace, and putting the next month's meals in the deep freeze. Anthony Powell and Angus Wilson will be popping in for drinks soon to read me advance proofs of their rave reviews of my first novel, and later the Rolling Stones, Geoff Boycott, Goldie Hawn, Iris Murdoch, Giulini, Mary Whitehouse, Ken Russell, Mr Ryland, Mr Jackson, nice Lord Hall and Robert Graves will be joining us for an intimate little dinner. Robert's staying on a few days – he won't stop anywhere else when he's in London.

Yves is right – this dress with horizontal stripes does *suit* me; goodness, I really must take the home-made bread out of the oven. I wonder who's sent me four dozen red roses?

Embarrassing Moments

Are you squirming uncomfortably? – then I'll begin. My most humiliating experience occurred when I was seven – the day my first pony arrived. Having boasted about it for weeks, I dragged several classmates home to witness the touching first meeting. They hung over the gate as I rushed up to this adorable, fluffy animal and flung my arms round his neck. Whereupon he turned around and bit me viciously. The derisive giggling of my friends echoes in my ears to this day.

But generally as a child, I found dogs more blush-making than ponies: big dogs that sniffed, small dogs that mounted one's leg at polite tea parties, and our own retriever, who invariably mistook other people's pale-silk sofas for a lamp-post.

Many children are crippled with embarrassment by parents wearing the wrong clothes at speech day. Mine were blameless in this respect, but my father did make me curl up by singing the bass part in church. I was convinced everyone must be staring at the little girl who was standing next to the big man singing the wrong tune.

Being lousy at games or, even worse, gym was also a constant source of humiliation. Thundering the length of the gymnasium with the whole class smirking and knowing you hadn't a hope of clearing that loathsome box; or the misery of team games, when two girls would pick sides and you were the last person left so you had to slink to one side unchosen.

Being in love is fraught with embarrassment. I blush to remember how one of my great loves told my best friend (who promptly told me) that I kissed like a vacuum cleaner. It put me off men for years. But I still giggle over the discomfort of the man who tried to pick me up in the Tube one morning and was appalled to find me sitting next to him at a dinner party that evening when he turned up with his intensely imposing wife.

My husband doesn't embarrass me very often, although twice at respectable parties he's sat on antique occasional tables and shattered them like matchwood. And when he's tight he's inclined to lie on his back and pretend he's a bear, although he usually confines this to the privacy of his own home.

I know I embarrass my husband by making too much noise when I get overexcited, by reading in the street and bumping into lamp-posts and by always looking immediately, whenever he says, 'Don't look now, but . . .'

Being caught in the wrong of course is always embarrassing. A letter came for my husband the other morning from a very rich relation. Not being able to contain myself, I opened and read it, noted with relief and delight it contained a fat cheque and carefully sealed it up again. Later, my husband came home and went through his mail. 'Maggie must be going senile,' I heard him say irritably. 'She says she's sent me a cheque but she's forgotten to put it in.'

I froze with horror to see the cheque lying on the kitchen table; in my haste to seal up the letter I'd forgotten to put it back.

But my favourite caught-in-the-act story comes from a producer I know who was driving through Hollywood one arctic night when he saw a naked man loping along the street and flagging him down for a lift.

'What on earth happened to you?' asked my friend.

'Oh,' said the naked man, 'the husband came back.'

Another thing I find embarrassing is when people ring up at half an hour's notice and want to come and stay, and the sheets are all in the laundry basket and the towels – because we haven't bought any new ones since we were married – are all in holes and the texture of Brillo pads.

I am also embarrassed staying in other people's houses if they don't put locks on the loo door. Or at parties when you turn up in scruff order and everyone else is done up to the tens. Or when you faint from the heat and everyone assumes you're pregnant or drunk or both. I also hate being made a fool of in public. I never know what to do with my face when men in Tyrolean dress come and sing at me in nightclubs; or at the pantomime when Dick Whittington's cat comes padding purposefully down the aisle and drags me on to the stage to be sawn in half or wave handkerchiefs.

My mother tells me that her most embarrassing moment was when she screwed herself up to have a blazing row with my brother's housemaster and, having routed him on every count, she swept out of his study. It was only when she was halfway down the stairs she discovered she'd left her knitting ball behind and she had to follow the trail of wool all the way back to his study to collect it.

Finally: to cap all embarrassment stories, a friend of mine was in London for the day and suddenly saw a woman sitting opposite her in the Tube wearing exactly the same hat – red felt with a blue band. She started giggling at the woman and pointing at her own hat. The woman looked very tight-lipped and moved down the carriage, so my friend grinned round at everyone else and kept pointing at her hat.

No one grinned back. Most of them stared fixedly out of the window. Several got out at the next stop. It was only when she got out several stations later, and caught a glimpse of herself in a shop window, that my friend realised what was the matter. In her haste to leave home she had put on her green beret instead of her red hat with the blue band.

A Deadly Sin

The deadly sin I have the most trouble with is Gluttony. Every morning, on waking, I finger my rolls of superfluous flesh and vow that today will herald the dawn of a newer, slimmer Cooper.

It never works. Every evening, I go to bed a sadder and a wider woman, acutely conscious of having eaten too much, racked by fantasies about becoming the fat lady in a circus, or being doomed to an eternity of tastefully draped V-necked dresses from Evans the Outsize Shop.

The reasons for my predicament are threefold. First, I adore food; second, I am devoid of self-control; and third, the moment I feel bored, unhappy or frustrated, I start eating. The slightest setback: a cross word from my husband or one of the cats, an abusive letter from the Gas Board, a friend cutting me in the street, sends me post haste to the bread bin and the marmalade pot.

A quick rundown on my cronies gets the same answer. 'As soon as my lover went to Spain,' said one girl, 'I started gorging myself.' 'Greed comes over me like a terrible sexual compulsion whenever I feel low,' said another. 'I don't even taste what I'm eating, I just keep on. Every time my husband goes to pick up his children from his first wife I wolf a whole packet of biscuits.'

It seems a pity the manufacturers can't package self-control instead of those nasty slimming biscuits which taste like cement between two pieces of blotting paper or those revolting sweetening tablets that make a perfectly good cup of coffee undrinkable.

My husband, who lost over a stone when he gave up drinking for six weeks, believes it's alcohol that puts on the weight. But I think it's the fact that drink undermines one's good resolutions. Once I get a few gin and tonics inside me I think: to hell with slimming, men like a nice cosy armful anyway. Then I head straight for the salted almonds.

My more affluent friends cope with the slimming problem by having appetite-killing injections, living on meat and citrus fruits and, as a result, becoming terrible drags to have to dinner. Or else they steal off to Entrail Hall and return ten days later, irrigated at every orifice, thinner, paler and demonstrably smugger. I have toyed with the idea of joining them, but some miserly streak in my nature rebels against paying a fortune for ten days' starvation. Cheaper to buy a padlock for the fridge.

And all those different diets. You name it, I've tried it and haven't stuck to it. Slimming exercises are no good either because they make my husband howl with laughter. I've tried pasting photographs of girls in bikinis on all the biscuit tins, I have even hung a large mirror in the kitchen so that I can stare at myself every time I start eating. I look so disgusting it worked at first, but I'm now inured even to that.

It's quite impossible to slim in our house because no one sets me a good example. The cat is pregnant and is eating for at least a dozen. Time and again, I've cooked three courses for a dinner party the following night, and come into the kitchen to find my husband scoffing the lot. And our lodger is just like the charwoman in the N. F. Simpson play who came in every day to finish up the leftovers: 'I've eaten the rice pudding and the fish pie, but I haven't been able to manage the steak and kidney pudding.'

And why is one so ashamed of being overweight? – ripping out the size 14 label before showing off a new dress to the rest of the office – or, like a friend of mine, always explaining her plumpness to shop assistants by saying she hasn't got her figure back yet after the baby. Her children are ten and five.

And why are we so ashamed of gluttony? The number of bright conversations I've carried on, desperately trying to conceal the fact that a chocolate biscuit is melting up my sleeve, or my cheeks are bulging with cold sprouts.

The fact is that nothing equals the bliss of losing weight, the sheer joy of being able to throw oneself down on somebody's lap without having to leave both feet on the ground to spread the load, or being lifted up by some playful admirer without his turning purple and the veins standing out on his forehead.

A friend of mine was so delighted to shed two stone that she went down to the butcher's and made him weigh out the equivalent in meat, so she could see what she had lost. 'It was wonderful,' she sighed afterwards. 'There were two legs of lamb, a small turkey, four pounds of liver and a mass of pork chops.'

Yet although I yearn to be *mince* myself, all the people I love most have large appetites, if not for food, then for drink or cigarettes or sex. And all my great loves in history or literature, Byron, Falstaff, Hamlet, Oscar Wilde and wicked old Henry VIII, seem also to have had a weight problem.

I admire self-control in others, but I'm far more seduced by self-indulgence. One of the things that endears my husband to me most is the way his lip trembles when he sees the last finger of whisky poured into someone else's glass.

But if you ever feel really low about being fat, turn to *Roget's Thesaurus*, and read what it says about being thin: 'THIN – spare, meagre, skinny, bony, cadaverous, fleshless, skin and bone, haggard, weedy, scrawny, lantern-jawed, hatchet-faced.'

Still want to slim?

On Being a Second Wife

I fell in love with my husband at a children's party when I was nine. A girl called Louise was rabbiting on about how many more acres her father had than anyone else's when my husband, then aged twelve, suddenly picked up a strawberry jelly and hurled it at her. His aim – as now – was true.

At school I wrote him rambling letters drenched in Evening in Paris ending 'I must stop now and go to choir practice.' At twenty-one he got married to someone else.

Six years later I met him by chance at a dinner party. His marriage had just broken up. He'd changed of course: tougher, more bitter, with a disconcerting habit of not laughing at my jokes, and of disagreeing with nine out of ten of my remarks. He referred constantly to his wife and the fact that she had left him.

I was extremely surprised when he asked me out the following night, and impressed and irritated that he didn't make a pass at me. On our second date we went to the theatre. Attempting to look sophisticated, I'd had my hair put up at vast expense. Much later that evening when he'd taken every pin out of my hair, he said I was never to put it up again as he decided he wanted to marry me. It seemed a good idea. There was just the question of his getting divorced from his wife.

At the time it didn't worry me that he'd been married before. It gave him glamour, mystery, an aura of tragedy. I would be the ministering angel that soothed away the pain and restored his faith in human nature. There were tremendous advantages, too. Not only did he have experience but also furniture and kitchen utensils. Instead of pots and pans and toast racks, I could ask for pianos and Staffordshire dogs for wedding presents.

I hardly gave his first wife a thought. Anyone stupid enough to leave someone as lovely as him I felt wasn't worth considering. We had an idyllic summer playing hide-and-seek with the Queen's Proctor and taking my husband's daughter, then aged five, to the zoo on Saturdays. We were married in the autumn.

Trouble began soon afterwards, when he delivered his daughter back to his first wife one evening. He returned looking pale and unhappy. 'She was looking very pretty,' he admitted later. 'She gave me that special sideways look under her eyelashes and I wanted her like hell.'

Although I was knocked for six, I don't think I made an issue of it at the time.

A few weeks later she rang up. I answered the telephone. In a husky, I thought consciously sexy voice she asked if she might speak to my husband. They gossiped for three-quarters of an hour, by which time I had been reduced to tears.

I began to worry that he never said anything derogatory about her. 'At least it means if you leave him he won't bitch about you,' said a friend, which didn't help much.

Little by little, this first wife was becoming an obsession. Suddenly her possessions seemed to litter the flat, sheets with her name tapes on, books with her name written inside – they all appeared to be Bibles or prayer books – address books of people they had both known, anthologies with love poems underlined, old dress patterns, scent bottles, odd shoes.

Whenever my husband went out, I ransacked his desk, lacerating myself reading old love letters she had written him, or letters he had written her and never posted.

Jealousy gnawed at me for those years they'd spent together. Had he only married me to staunch the wound, because he needed a housekeeper, a hostess at his table, because I adored him and because he fancied me? My obsession was driving me into prolonged black moods. I kept making plans to wait in a café outside her flat in north London so, unbeknown to her, I could see what she was really like.

My husband decided it might help if I met her. So, on Christmas Eve, we called in for a cup of coffee. Determined to appear as though I did this sort of thing every day, I'd spent all afternoon putting on my make-up to look as though I wasn't wearing any.

She, by contrast, looked like the Queen of the Night – black sweater, black leather skirt, fishnet stockings, jet earrings, black nail polish and lashings of black eye make-up. We sat round being excessively polite, studying each other when we thought the other wasn't looking. I'd never reckoned she'd be that attractive. She seemed to thrum with sex.

We had a merry Christmas after that with me in tears most of the time. I knew I was being selfish, and it didn't help realising that my misery was motivated more by furious jealousy than by worry that he might still be in love with her.

Was she better in bed than me? I kept asking my husband. She was different, he replied tactfully.

Another distressing factor was that I couldn't have children, and in five years while I ricocheted from one specialist to another, she remarried and went on to produce four more children.

The first two years I was married were the worst. Our fourth wedding anniversary was a landmark – it meant I had been married to my husband longer than she had.

Then she went to America and later we heard she was separating from her second husband to marry a third. At least I was better at staying married than she was.

Ironically, what really laid the ghost was my falling in love three years ago with another man who fell in love with me to such an extent that it rocked my marriage to its foundations. After appalling unhappiness on all sides, the whole thing blew over, having taught me what I wanted to know all the time – that my husband really loved me, needed me and would have been devastated if I'd left him.

It also made me realise that my husband's first wife was not a man-eater, nor a monster of depravity, but merely a woman who had fallen in love with someone else while she was married.

Last October we adopted a baby. It has been an unqualified success, and has put the final nail in the coffin of my obsession.

Christmas Cards

I always try to pretend Christmas doesn't exist – like an amorous drunk on the late-night Tube.

Why should I be sucked into the festive whirl? I whine. Why should I be pressurised into sending hundreds of Christmas cards?

But come December the heat is on. The first cards come drifting in from abroad and the lighted tree goes up in the house opposite, blazing green, red and white at mind-blowing two-second intervals through the night. Its only advantage is that it guides us home after parties like the Eddystone lighthouse.

My *angst* increases as local cards pour in and as I see my neighbours waddling smugly down to the post office, their arms full of envelopes. 'Got your tree up?' they shout. 'Baby's going to enjoy Christmas this year.'

I usually hold out grimly until Christmas Eve, when I rush out to find all the decent cards sold, and I have to make do with spangled horrors wishing the folks at home sincere seasonal greetings in loopy gold writing. These will arrive in time to wish everyone a Happy New Year, or lie around on the hall table for weeks with names but no addresses, because my son has ripped the relevant page out of the telephone book.

The trouble with Christmas cards is that they are so expensive. I suppose one could use ink eradicator on last year's cards – one stylish chum crosses out the names on cards he has received and sends them out again like a chain letter.

There are people who try to get round the problem by advertising in the Personal Column the fact that they are not sending cards. They then bankrupt themselves by ringing all their friends to check that they have seen the ad.

This year we have had a fairly representative bunch of cards: etchings of Christmas roses from aunts, potato cuts from the artistic, postcards of Old Masters which fall over, olive branches from the contrite, cards from creditors wistfully wishing us a prosperous New Year.

It fascinates me the way the same themes recur over the years. Here is our Top Ten so far this year:

Festive robins, 20; Mufflered snowmen, 19; Regimental crests, 17; Cottage with light in snowy dell, 16; Jolly cardinals drinking indifferent claret in front of a roaring fire, 12; Old Masters, 10; Puffed-cheek Dickensian trumpeters, 9; Santa and his reindeer crew, 8; Pheasants in flaming bracken, 7; Wise Men, 5.

Tip for the top: Blessed Virgins, after a slow start moving up fast and looks like being a real chart-buster.

We have also had a number of cards from people with illegible handwriting. 'Who the hell are Duck and Piggy?' says my husband. 'Some bizarre chums of yours, I suppose.'

'Dick and Peggy,' I snap, 'are that awfully nice couple who took us stock car racing. We must do something about them . . .' Up goes their card, and we forget about them for another twelve months. We always have at least six unidentifiable cards from people called John.

I can never understand the mentality of people who hang their cards on clothes lines across the room. I cover every available piece of furniture with ours – it is such a marvellous excuse not to have to dust for a month.

I must admit that even though I hate the bother of sending cards, I would be livid not to get any myself. There is a terrific one-upmanship about who has the most and the best cards. Have you noticed how people bring their cards back from the office at weekends to swell the home team, and how they leave the ones from Jackie and Ari or Elizabeth and Philip open at an obtuse angle at the front?

One chum keeps all his cards from years back and whenever he wants to impress anyone with his popularity unearths a couple of hundred old cards and puts them up beside the current year's intake.

We have kept all our cards, too, since we married, hoping with true Bandalog fervour that one day we would cover a screen with the prettiest ones. Leafing through them the other day, I was appalled how many people we have known and let slip through our fingers like minnows, but also fascinated by the progress of their lives.

In 1964, for example, we get a card 'from Gideon and the lads at No. 51'. In 1965, Gideon is married and we get a card from Gideon and Samantha.

1966 – love from Gideon, Samantha and Dominic (aged two months).

1967 – love from Gideon, Samantha, Dominic, Jeremy and Sue (twins!).

1968 – obviously too poor to send cards.

1969 – overwhelmed with parental responsibility, Gideon walks out.

1970 – Gideon shacks up with his secretary, and it starts again: love from Gideon and Denise.

I do wish Christmas-card manufacturers would be more imaginative about their verse instead of all that snow and jingle bells and 'hearty greetings brimful of cheer to someone dear'. My husband was so enraged by the banality of this year's offerings that he composed a little poem which I feel constitutes a real breakthrough in Christmas verse:

> *'Noel,' the festive Robin cried,*
> *When he the heavenly babe espied.*
> *But Santa said: 'Enough of that.'*
> *And with a yule log squashed him flat.*

A Merry Christmas to you all.

Between Covers

My second-favourite pleasure in the world is reading. Like Charles Lamb, I love to lose myself in other men's minds. When I am not talking, I have my nose buried in a book – I am quite incapable of sitting and thinking.

When I was a child I used to read as I cycled back and forth to school. Fortunately I only travelled deserted moorland tracks, but even so I fell in the beck twice and several sheep had very narrow escapes. I shudder to think what the local paper would have made of such an accident: 'BOOK-WORM RAMS EWES,' I suppose.

I have very catholic tastes in reading matter – anything from Homer to the bit on the Harpic tin about 'If the bowl is encrusted with lime', which I've read so often I know it by heart. But I'm an imperfect reader – I can get through a whole novel in an evening and not remember a character from it two days later.

When I go into other people's houses the first thing I look at is their books. If they haven't got any, I immediately want to go home again. I'm not too happy in country houses either, where all you can find is shelves devoted to *Coarse Fishing* and *Your Compleat Hound*, and endless unread leather-bound volumes of Walter Scott. Or girls' flats where the only literature consists of *The Valley of the Dulls, A Son Is My Undoing, Love Has Wings* by Barbara Carthorse and that copy of *Teach Yourself Turkish* which Jennifer bought after she met that fisherman in Cyprus.

It always amuses me, too, what books people give one to read. Last time we went away for the weekend, our hostess put *Married Love* and some rubbish about *The Sensual Wombat* by my bed, and then had the temerity to put us in separate rooms.

The houses I'm happiest in are those which have masses of books which really look as though they're being used. Books should be tattered and fingered, double-parked on shelves, corrugated from being dropped in the bath. The greatest compliment you can pay an author is to read and reread his book until it falls to pieces.

I'm so pig-headed, I never read a book if someone tells me I simply *must* read it. That's why censorship is so stupid –

the quickest way to get a child to read something is to tell it not to. I still remember the guilty thrill of reading *Dandy* and *Beano* and Oscar Wilde with a torch under the bedclothes.

With notable exceptions, I'm not crazy about book reviews these days. Finding a mention of the book concerned in some of those long pieces is like looking for a needle in a haystack. And why do they waste 3,000 words on some Ceylonese translation of Wittgenstein – a specialist book which the specialists will all buy anyway – when they could cover fifteen different really worthwhile titles in the same space, books which will probably never get reviewed at all.

And why do reviewers use such long words? I was wildly excited recently when a reviewer described something I'd written as tumescent. I thought it meant sexy. Then I looked it up in the dictionary and discovered it means bombastic, inflated, swollen. So much for my tumescent head!

But to return to reading, I am constantly amazed by how many people consider it rather a decadent pastime. Those awful women – *Good Housekeeping* seals usually – who say so smugly: 'Oh I never get time to read,' as though there were some merit in the fact they spend their evenings making bread and running up curtains.

And why do people think it is so much more virtuous to read biographies than novels? Most novels are biographical anyway. Novelists are so busy writing about their friends and enemies that usually the only line of fiction in their whole book is the bit at the beginning about: 'None of the characters bears any resemblance to any living person.'

I think one of the main reasons I'm such a voracious reader is because I don't get the chance to bury my nose in a book all the time. The most boring job I ever had was two years in publishing when I was employed to sit in a little office reading manuscripts all day, and recommending them or not for publication.

How dismally I discovered that there is indeed a book in everyone: 'I'm sure you will enjoy this not unhumorous account of my twenty-six years in the Pioneer Corps.' Or: 'My colleagues at work have persuaded me to send my little collection of verses to you. I have a number of friends in Cambridge who will certainly buy the book.' Oh my paws and whiskers!

My favourite line came out of a submitted novel: 'He kissed her passionately without taking his pipe out of his mouth.' Talk about a burning embrace.

To begin with I felt sorry for these would-be authors, and wrote them nice letters about changing the odd word, and having better luck with other publishers. But inevitably their manuscripts came back by return of post with one word altered, and they would be furious when once again I would reject them. I was also foolish enough to write to one man and say I'd enjoyed his sex bits. From then on he kept sending me photographs of himself with nothing on. After that I resorted to rejection slips.

I think what I like best about books is that they are all things to all moods. You can read poetry when you're in love, Anthony Powell when you want to meet a few amusing people, Nancy Mitford when you need a good giggle. Montaigne when you want your sanity restored.

At the end of the Six-Day War under the dust and rubble in one of the Egyptian trenches was found a Russian translation of *Eugénie Grandet*. It made me ridiculously happy somehow to imagine that some young handsome Russian officer, perhaps slightly homesick, or frightened, or more likely bored by a tedious foreign war, found escape and consolation in Balzac.

On the Move

We had to move – we'd run out of space. The cats had reached the age when they really needed a room of their own, and my husband was fed up with treading on pieces of Lego every time he got up in the morning.

So we found a heavenly house just off Putney Common, with masses of room and garden, and by some miracle managed to raise a mortgage. We even sold our Fulham house painlessly. But once over the euphoria of finding a new place, we were faced with the inevitable hell of moving houses at top speed.

Like most women, I detest change, and the prospect of being torn out by the roots fills me with horror. I know I shall adore Putney once I get settled in, but I couldn't bear the thought of leaving dear, dear Fulham.

The act of packing up is so disrupting. I kept packing things I needed, and for the last three weeks before we moved, I found myself blubbing over the smallest thing – *Anne of Green Gables* on telly, or the yellow crocuses defying the icy February wind outside my son's playschool.

And where would I find another playschool as cosy, or an off-licence who let me run up bills in three figures, or a launderette where they bring my washing round to the house when I forget it, or a bank and a chemist who don't mind cheques or prescriptions caked in liver blood or spilt make-up?

Then there is the terrible palaver of dealing with the various boards. Their product may be high-speed, but you have to put a bomb under the Gas Board to get them to do anything, particularly now they're out converting everyone to North Sea Gas with more than Catholic zeal.

'I've got a young baby with a weak chest,' I pleaded. 'I must have hot water before we move in.'

'Everyone gives us that story, madam,' said the Gas Board official wearily.

And the Electricity Board would turn up and rabbit on like Mr Darcy about the inferiority of my connections.

Then there's that awful measuring for carpets and curtains. The only thing I can measure with any efficiency is my length after parties. One also becomes boringly obsessed with colour combinations. Little bits of material lie round the house, and I can't pass a traffic light without wondering whether amber would go well with red in one of the children's bedrooms.

On the Thursday, however, the chaos really set in, when a removal man arrived with fifty paper sacks, so we could pack all our books and ornaments before the move proper.

On Thursday afternoon, someone turned up to remove the drawing-room carpet, a new nanny came for an interview, followed by two advertising men who might put me in a commercial. I was so much on the blink by then, I kept getting everyone confused and telling the ad men I did hope they were kind to adults as well as children, and what days off did they want, and did they expect me to pay their stamps.

On Friday I did some sorting out, which meant transferring marbles and old mascara brushes and Brooke Bond picture cards of dinosaurs and mastodons from one glass bowl on the kitchen shelf to another. I also tried and failed to throw a few things away – ribbons, for example. I'm far too old to wear ribbons in my hair, but perhaps our baby daughter might need them in a few years. Should I keep a leaflet on fondue parties? Hell, I would never give a fondue party in my life – into the dustbin at once. Five minutes later, I about-faced. Who knows, I might become famous in Putney for my fondue parties. I delved down in the dustbin to retrieve the leaflet, which was now drenched in mushroom soup from a leaking tin.

On Saturday, we all packed frenziedly, except my son, who frenziedly unpacked everything we packed. As the rooms were stripped of books, ornaments and pictures, it was as though we were playing a reel of film backwards. The house began to look more and more as it did when we first moved in. In the middle of the afternoon we all had to preserve ninety minutes' silence while my husband watched the Rugger International.

A mate turned up to help clean the kitchen.

'Is this a floor cloth?' she said, scrubbing the floor vigorously with one of my best scarves. 'It is now,' I said.

On Sunday, we took more mates over to see the new house. They rhapsodised, but I noticed they were a bit cautious in their comments as they entered each room, in case they expressed horror at the one place we'd just spent fortunes redecorating.

I decided to get a dog. I shall buy a trend setter I can take for walks on the common.

On the way home to Fulham, we passed the jellied eel stall, and I promptly started snivelling into a Kleenex again. 'But you hate jellied eels,' groaned my husband. 'I know,' I sobbed, 'but I might have learnt to love them.'

Monday – and D-Day. The removal men descended like locusts. Within two minutes they had packed my first draft of this piece. No doubt I shall discover it in six months' time.

'We're trained to pack everything,' said the foreman, shovelling my most frivolous underwear into a packing case without turning a hair. Any moment I imagined he would gather me up, slap a page of the *Daily Mirror* round me and shove me in as well.

I had decided it would be easier to clean up after everything was removed. Alas the gas and electricity people in their wisdom had turned everything off, so there was no hot water, and no power to run the Hoover. The cats had all bolted. It was like the last act of *The Cherry Orchard*.

I rode in the removal van to the new house, which was absolutely freezing. The Gas Board still hadn't got round to turning on the heating. The baby's nose was as red as a cherry. My husband stood in the hall, a glass of whisky in his hand, directing the placing of the furniture. I burrowed in the packing chests, frenziedly unpacking to discover the gin.

Our son was having a field day, he had already locked his grandmother in the potting shed, and two of the removal men in the cellar. The house was full of workmen. Our pretty nanny made endless cups of tea and was the target of much dungaree bonhomie.

It was getting colder. My husband went off to get some plugs. 'I may be gone some time,' he said, spoiling his Captain Oates exit by tripping over the intestines of the grandfather clock.

The gas men miraculously arrived, then read the instructions for conversion, their lips moving, running their fingers along the lines. Any moment, like Lady Eden, I felt the North Sea would be flowing through my drawing room. The flame flickered, we all jumped back nervously, we were converted.

My son was busy telling a removal man to put the sideboard in the downstairs lavatory. I tried to hang a few temporary curtains. They looked all wrong, like midi dresses. I have a feeling we shall be camping for months – I must be horribly deficient in Girl Guide spirit.

No one could find the baby's nappies, or the tin opener. I lost one of my only wearable pairs of shoes. Two of the cats had been rounded up and, having acupunctured my knees in the car all the way over, were now sitting morosely in a kitchen cupboard, rejecting a great plate of liver. We unpacked and unpacked, and argued where things should go. Finally we gave up and went out for a very alcoholic dinner.

We still hadn't found our little black cat. On the way back to the new house, we stopped off at the old house to try and catch her. There were no lights on, and although the rooms were flooded with moonlight, they already seemed filled with ghosts. Out in the garden, the blocks of flats beyond hung like Chinese lanterns. My voice echoed forlornly and absurdly round the houses, calling the cat's name.

I was about to give up, when a little black shadow slipped out from under the lilac tree and rubbed against my legs. She was shivering. I felt she understood how wretchedly displaced I was feeling. Some gin-induced tears were shed, then hand in paw, with wandering steps and slow, out of Fulham, we took our solitary way.

Here Lies Jilly Cooper

I got myself into a muddle recently. A nice eager lady from the BBC rang up and asked me to appear on *Woman's Hour*. Greatly honoured, I agreed. It was only as she rang off, she added that the programme was being recorded in Birmingham.

This put a different complexion on the matter – to Broadcasting House from Putney takes only half an hour; but a trip to Birmingham means a whole work day lost, not to mention meals and magazines and those two pounds I have always to spend in station chemists whenever I go by train.

So I wrote a polite lying letter saying I was heartbroken, but I'd suddenly discovered I had to be in Bristol that day. Return of post comes a telephone call – saying, that was fine, as I was going to be in Bristol, could I record the programme from the BBC studios there?

It was too shaming. But then my husband says I'm incapable of telling the truth, and that I ought to have a plaque on the front of the house saying, 'Here Lies Jilly Cooper'. I kid myself I'm not deliberately dishonest, just born in Pisces, which means, according to my horoscope book, one lies out of general confusion.

Then I remember the times recently I've rung people pretending I've got 'flu, merely because it's a nice day, and I wanted to sit in the sun rather than go out. Another great excuse is: 'I must have eaten something', or 'struck down by shellfish'. As soon as someone mentions that word 'gastric' you know they're lying.

Thank God at least for the bath: 'Jilly can't talk now, she's in the bath' or 'She's bathing the children' (usually at some quite improbable hour like 1.45), or 'Jilly and Leo are in the bath' (implying sexual junketing – on no account to be disturbed. People must think we're the cleanest family in Putney).

With such an example it's hardly surprising my children are raving mythomaniacs: my son blaming the three-day week as the reason he hasn't put his toys away, my daughter having scribbled all over the non-wash wallpaper, blaming it on the dog.

But then I'm not sure a truthful nature equips one for life *these* days. Good secretaries seem to spend all day lying on behalf of their bosses, and one is constantly being told of bright young things who 'bluffed' their way into a marvellous job, which is merely a euphemism for a pack of lies.

Odd, too, when one lies so often, how embarrassed one is to be caught out, like a friend of mine who said she couldn't lunch with a man because she was on a diet, then later that day went slap into him in the King's Road just as she was stuffing a large cream bun into her face.

Then there was the memorable occasion when my brother, who had been borrowing my aunt's car, told her he had had the brakes checked but actually forgot to do it. And in horrified amusement, he watched her gathering speed down the main road into the village, finally landing up like Ferdinand the Bull surrounded by cinerarias in the front window of the local flower shop.

I don't lie about my age yet – but I do about the dog's, pretending he's younger than he is to justify such rumbustious behaviour. And although my daughter's three next week, I tell everyone she's two, in the hope that people will say how forward she is. My great friend, however, has a daughter, who from her seventeenth birthday has been described as nearly eighteen, so everyone gasps and says: 'You can't possibly have a daughter of eighteen.'

Equally I always tell people we've lived in the house less time than we actually have because I feel guilty we haven't done more to it.

Some people lie about their backgrounds – making them grander than they were – but as they become more successful they tend to be less reticent about their humble origins so that people will be even more impressed by the distance they've climbed.

Liking to appear sensitive, I always pretend I was more unhappy at school than I really was, and I went through a stage of telling people my father was a scientist rather than an engineer because it sounded more boffinish and romantic.

I was always brought up to be truthful. It must be marriage that made a dishonest woman of me.

If we're going out in the evening, and I ring up to find out the time, I always report that it's ten minutes earlier than it really is, so my husband won't harass me. But then if he rings up, he always says it's ten minutes later to panic me into getting a move on.

Once people are separated they embark on a new set of lies – trying to convince each other how little the other is living on, sending the children over in clean but heavily darned clothes, leaving the Bentley round the corner and arriving on foot.

A friend of mine wanted to wear his new suede jacket when he took his girlfriend over to his ex-wife to collect the children, but was nervous his wife would think he was wasting maintenance money on new clothes. So his girlfriend suggested he should say that she bought it for him.

Sure enough the moment they arrived the wife's eyes zoomed in on the new jacket.

'Angela bought it for me,' blurted out the husband, adding hastily, 'It was frightfully cheap.'

People lie about the number of people they've been to bed with, men generally bumping up the number. Women, rather like birds, don't seem able to count beyond three. Women lie about their weight and dyeing their hair. Men lie about the time they spend getting from A to B. If they've been drinking in the pub, they always spend 'hours' stuck in traffic jams getting home.

Recently we were lent a Rolls-Royce, worth £17,000, for the weekend. We drove it up to Yorkshire, where my husband and I both grew up. It would have been so easy to pass it off to all our childhood friends as our own. Instead we found ourselves falling over backwards to tell everyone – even policemen checking tyres – that it had only been lent. I think it was the splendour and true-blue nature of the car which brought out the latent George Washington in both of us.

Actually George Washington must have been a pain in the ashlar, if he really couldn't tell a lie. He certainly wouldn't have lasted in politics today.

In fact the official lie has become so commonplace, one hardly notices it: Anthony Eden denying there was collusion between the French and the Israelis over Suez; categorical denials that Pompidou was dying or that the Prime Minister's private secretary was going to be given a seat in the Lords; Buckingham Palace flatly denying there was anything between Princess Anne and Mark Phillips. We seem to be suffering from galloping mendacity.

Waxing Lyrical

Some of my best friends are poets. I would rather spend an afternoon with Chatterton or Keats than with most people of my acquaintance. I am far more excited by a shelf full of verse than a room full of people. In a way, poetry takes the place of religion in my life. Instead of rushing to the Bible for comfort and inspiration I pick up a copy of Milton or Shakespeare.

I realise, however, it is a passion that lays me open to ridicule. I suppose that is why it is called po-wet-try. People consider it very soppy to be always reading poems or spouting quotations. My family, for example, used to send me up rotten when I was a child.

One of my favourite sonnets was Keats' 'On First Looking into Chapman's Homer'. But my father pointed out the bit about 'Stout Cortez silent upon a peak in Darien', so now I have this picture of some poor dog yapping and flattened beneath an overweight and contemplative pioneer.

Then our next-door neighbour had a ginger tom, called Hopkins, but after it was neutered, my brother christened it Gerard Unmanly . . . and so it went on. Not the sort of atmosphere where poetic natures flourished.

Despite this I have an aunt who has written a great deal of poetry and gets it published all over the place. There was considerable tut-tutting in the family circle many years ago when she circulated a poem to relations young and old which began: 'I have raped the chambers of knowledge.'

At school we got very excited over Horatius and Sir Lancelot with his coal-black curls streaming under his helmet. And we were deeply moved by Sir Richard Grenville and the little *Revenge* – they had the same sort of giant-killer appeal as the brilliant young showjumper Marion Coakes and her adorable pony, Stroller.

Then at fifteen we were unleashed on the Romantic poets, and all our unidentified adolescent longings found an outlet. We weren't allowed much Byron – I think they were scared we might inquire about his private life. But we adored 'Kubla Khan', particularly the bit about: 'As if this earth in fast thick pants were breathing,' which reminded us of our blue serge gym knickers. And Shelley's 'Adonais' affected us like a fever:

'He has outsoared the shadow of our night. Envy and cal-
umny and hate and pain . . .'

Most of the poems we learnt seemed to come from Palgrave's not so *Golden Treasury*, which contains far too much
Thomas Campbell and other rubbish, but no Donne. I suppose Palgrave considered him too acid and tortuous.

When I reached my typing school in Oxford, however,
Donne had suddenly become wildly fashionable, and every
undergraduate without fail would quote: 'Oh my America
my new-found-land,' before he pounced on one.

After leaving typing school, I worked on a local paper,
and never went anywhere without clutching some volume
of poetry, which usually had to double up as a reporter's
notebook. To this day on the title page of my copy of *The
Wreck of the Deutschland* is scribbled a shorthand description of a scrap-metal theft, while underneath Auden's
poem about Rimbaud and Verlaine is scrawled a police-
man's evidence during a court case: 'I was proceeding
along the footway when I saw the defendant sitting in a
gutter. He said: "I am Humpty Dumpty, I bet you cannot
put me together again," and I formed the opinion he was
drunk.'

But I suppose poetry ultimately appeals most when one is in love. One husband I know says he can always tell when his wife is having an affair, because all the poetry books are suddenly horizontal on top of the shelves.

I certainly read most voraciously during my adolescence and early twenties when I was hunting for a permanent mate, and ricocheting from one disastrous love affair to another. Only in poetry could I find appropriate expression for my ecstasy, or for my subsequent despair when things went wrong: 'Oh heart, oh, heart, if he'd but turn his head. You'd know the folly of being comforted.'

Actually I must have been a pain in the neck. 'You write wonderful letters, Jill,' I remember one stockbroker saying after receiving one of my lyrical outpourings, 'but they're awfully hard to answer.'

I confess I find it embarrassing myself when people start quoting at me, and even worse when they give me one of their poems to read. There's that terrible moment when you get to the bottom of the page, and they're watching you and you don't know if the poem's finished, or if there's more over the page. (You feel you ought to know from the sense.) So you turn over surreptitiously and find nothing, and have to pretend you're examining the quality of the paper.

I wish, too, I didn't always say: 'Gosh yes, it's wonderfully moving,' when I get to the end, even if I think it's frightful. I wish I were like Ezra Pound, who when Yeats sent him a poem, merely sent back a postcard saying: 'Putrid. E.P.'

I've always, too, been fascinated by the process of writing poetry. Does inspiration strike suddenly? How spontaneous really is the overflow of powerful feeling? We know Shakespeare never blotted a line, but did Wordsworth go charging round that Lakeland cottage, shouting: 'What the bloody hell rhymes with daffodils? Fetch me the rhyming dictionary, Dorothy.' I find it very endearing that Auden's secretary once typed the wrong adjective in a poem because she couldn't read his writing, and Auden was so delighted with the improvement he left it in.

'The chief, if not the only, aim of poetry is to delight,' wrote Dryden. And I think it's a pity that parents don't encourage their children to read poetry. In fact I think children should be forcibly introduced to it like being made to learn the piano, because it's such a joy and a consolation in later life, and it enables one to do the *Times* crossword so much quicker.

And poetry does comfort and cheer. I remember going to work one morning. I had just arrived in London, and, desperately homesick for Yorkshire, crossed in love, soaked by the rain on the way to the Tube and buffeted by commuters, I was eventually disgorged on to the platform. Opposite me on the wall was a Whitbread poster, a painting of the countryside with robins in the trees, and underneath as a caption some of Wordsworth's loveliest lines: 'Art thou the bird whom men love best. The pious bird with the scarlet breast. Our little English robin.'

And suddenly the dark dismal morning seemed full of light.

Scrimping and Scraping

After a spine-chilling bank statement yesterday, all my energies are now centred on a major panic about money. And these panics always take the same form. Last night I sweated into the still watches planning drastic economies and a complete change of lifestyles. About 4 a.m. I woke my husband: 'I've found the answer,' I said. 'I'm going to learn to drive at once and take the car to Sainsbury's every week and stock up and then . . .'

'I know, I know,' he muttered groggily, 'we're going to forget about wine, drink nothing but cider for the next six months, and have all the cats put down,' and promptly went back to sleep again.

After a wretched night, I spent a hideous day stewing windfalls, slicing the garlic sausage thinner, trying to persuade the children to eat margarine, and making a disgustingly fatty casserole out of belly of pork, which even the dog rejected.

I even washed and ironed four double sheets. I ironed and ironed and ironed and then discovered the beastly things had been trailing in the cat's plate, so the next guest who comes to stay will be wafted to sleep on the aroma of fish skin and nourishing jellymeat Whiskas.

I also made pathetic attempts to economise on telephone calls by trying to make my conversations terse and to the point. It didn't work.

'What's up with you?' said a girlfriend. 'You sound terribly ratty.'

So I had to invite her round for a drink to placate her, which meant another sortie to the off-licence. Our drink bills, I'm afraid, are astronomical. We've always had a better eye for a bar than a bargain.

And then, of course, there's loathsome Christmas looming on the horizon waiting to take another great bite out of the budget. If I could only give up gin and Christmas for a few years, we might keep our heads above water.

But alas my economy drives never last very long. After a week of shallow baths and turning off lights, the wine and cream start creeping back into the casseroles, and things return to normal.

Another reason we're broke is that since we moved over the river, we've had to make such an effort keeping up with the Joneses. In Fulham everyone kept to themselves, so we were able to live in complete squalor, but in Putney they're great droppers-in, so one has to keep the place clean, which means Hoovers roaring all the time, eating up electricity, and vats of Gumption and Flash and Safety Brobat arriving with every delivery from the grocer's. Cleanliness may be next to godliness, but it's very expensive.

Even worse, my children keep agitating for a colour telly, claiming nobody will come to play with them if they have to watch *Play School* in black and white.

We're also broke because we've got hooked on the fallacy that time is money. In fact it's just a marvellous excuse to take taxis everywhere rather than buses and, instead of trailing around the shops, to have everything delivered from the most expensive retailers in the Lower Richmond Road.

At least one gets Pink Stamps. But that doesn't help much. We've collected nearly forty books of stamps since we lived here, but when they showed us the catalogue the only thing we fancied out of a sea of chromium and plastic was a goat which turned out to be one of the props in the garden-tool section.

It isn't just the housekeeping that eats into the budget. Guilt costs a bomb. Every time I feel I've been neglecting my husband or the children, I spend a fortune on surprise presents, and I always overtip. It's part of my insecurity, that awful thing of wanting everyone in the world, even taxi drivers and porters, to love me.

Our house is a Gannetorium anyway. With six people in it, the roast joint always gets wolfed in a sitting and never graduates into cold meat or shepherd's pie.

My daily – who needs constant pandering to her kitchen-beautiful whims – keeps bullying me to invest in a deep freeze, claiming it's cheaper to buy in bulk. I'm resisting like hell. Bulk buying has never done anything but increase our bulk. Nobody has any self-control. The only thing a huge fridgeful of food would encourage would be midnight feasts.

The worst thing about being broke, however, is it causes so much marital discord. I know my attitude to money is irrational: complete flap when we haven't got any, complete refusal to talk about it because it's so boring when we have. My husband does his best to encourage me to budget. But we have these absurd squabbles when he comes home in the evening, finds three final demands growing mouldy beneath a pile of washing, and starts lecturing me about organisation and keeping bills in one place.

If, on the other hand, he's been overspending, I get the typical male bull about women not understanding economics, and money being a commodity that can be bought and sold like anything else.

I know I shouldn't grumble and that millions of people are far worse off than we are. But money does seem to have become impossibly tight recently since England joined the Common Market, and the Tories started living off the VAT of the land.

It seems rather immoral, too, that on the one hand wages are frozen, yet on the other, we are bombarded with Access Cards, credit facilities, round-the-clock cash dispensers and offers of easy terms – all encouraging us to spend more money and get deeper and deeper into debt.

There must be some solution to the problem. I have pipe dreams (I wonder if cardinals have Pope dreams) about being left a fortune or writing the great bestseller. But I think the answer would be to find a bisexual millionaire who would fall in love with me and my husband equally and take us on jaunts and pour money into the kitty – and into the kitties, too, for that matter. They'd much prefer steak tartare to Whiskas.

And I suppose there is some consolation to be gained from the fact that sex is still free. After all, it does keep one away from the shops some of the time.

Motherly Afflictions

As I ramble past the cemetery on Putney Common with the dog bounding irreverently in and out of the gravestones, one epitaph always catches my eye.

> *Jane Selwyn died 1889 – a devoted mother, her children arise and call her blessed.*

And I start wondering if the stonemasons will ever chisel such pleasantries on my tombstone. I rather doubt it.

I'd like to be a good mother. But it never seems to work that way with me. My children are angelic when they're asleep, and when my husband's there, but when I take them out on my own, they always seem to play up, running riot in Biba or letting water pistols loose on old ladies.

I took my son to the doctor yesterday. 'I'm terribly sorry to bother you,' I said with my usual string of apologies, 'but he's been boiling hot and he hasn't eaten for two days.'

'And I'm very hungry now,' announced my son, beaming.

You shouldn't spoil them, says my husband. I know, I know. But Emily, my daughter, has reached the stage when she wants to walk everywhere but refuses to hold my hand. The only way to keep her in her pram is bribery.

'I will not weaken,' I mutter grimly, as I trundle past the first sweet shop to the accompanying wails of 'lollies', 'sweeties'.

Come the second sweet shop, I invariably give in. Peace is restored with a large ice cream. Today, I tell myself guiltily, my sanity is more vital than Emily's character. Tomorrow I'll start saying no.

Then there are those dreadful afternoons when it's only three o'clock and pouring with rain, and there's no one for them to play with because all their friends are away. I turn into an instant fishwife. All I seem to be doing is screaming, and shouting: 'Stop it!' But the noise gets louder and louder, until finally it's tears before nightfall – usually mine. Where-upon there's a complete and shaming role reversal.

My daughter rushes over and starts patting me on the shoulder and saying sorry, and my son tries to placate me with a present.

Last week he consoled me with one of his Snap cards.

'What's the good of one lousy playing card?' I sniffed grudgingly.

'It's very good for picking your teeth,' said my son.

Then suddenly, in the middle of the night, the fishwife's remorse strikes (it should be turned into an opera by Benjamin Britten) when I wake up in a cold sweat and decide I'm ruining my children in their formative years, and all they'll remember when they grow up is my shouting at them. Comes the dawn, and still racked with doubt, I listen with blessed relief to the banging and singing upstairs as two apparently undamaged children greet a new day.

It's all to do with their ages, say kind friends. My son, being four, has reached the 'why' to everything stage, and my daughter at two wants to have long conversations, about half of which I understand. It's rather like having to talk French all day, and just as exhausting.

I think the trouble with our house is that too many people need a devoted mother. 'I never see you these days,' grumbles my husband. And the cats are so edgy since the dog arrived that I've had to evolve a stroking rota.

I thought it would be such a nice country atmosphere for the children if they were brought up with lots of animals – but all it means is discipline goes to pot at mealtimes.

How can I ensure my children eat up, when the dog is hanging around like a great grinning waste disposal unit, and the minute I look round, I'm confronted by two totally clean plates, and three innocent faces, except that the dog's cheeks are bulging with cold sprouts and pieces of sausage?

I don't even seem to have made a success of teaching my children the facts of life. I do try. But when I went upstairs the other day, I found my son cavorting round wearing a pair of my tights with two volumes of Walter Scott tucked in the front. My daughter lay on a sheet on the sofa, giggling.

'What are you both doing?' I said.

'We're playing fathers and daddies,' said my son.

I suppose, too, devoted mothers play with their children more than I do.

I like reading to them and telling them stories, but I really draw the line at Lego. My hands shake too much. Someone gave my son a huge box recently, and the house is now strewn with windowless bungalows – like an aftermath of the Bomb.

'It ought to be called Sore Footo, rather than Lego,' muttered my husband, as he staggered groggily out of bed this morning, treading hard on a half-built windmill.

But the thing I feel most angst-ridden about is not taking enough interest in my children's education. I glaze at dinner parties when the trendies start grumbling about this and Thatcher and the deficiencies of the state system.

You know the sort of thing.

'I wouldn't dream of letting Gideon go to a state school, and be jostled by all those rough children, besides they never push them enough.'

Equally depressing are the people who rush round putting foetuses down for Winchester or Cranborne Chase.

My children aren't down for anywhere. My son has just gone to the local primary school, which he refers to as All Scents. He adores it and he seems to enjoy all the 'jostling of the rough children'.

However, even that brought problems. There was no more rolling up at 10.30, like we used to at the Playgroup, when I had a hangover or overslept. The whistle goes promptly at 9.15.

Then there's the trauma of dinner money, 12p actually, to be found every day. I wanted to write a cheque, but evidently that's bad for discipline, so most mornings there's the same rat race of turning out piggy banks.

And I did hope at last the dreadful one-up-childship would let up, but it hasn't. Where it used to be 'Isn't he walking, talking, out of nappies yet?', it is now 'Gideon can read and write and count up to a thousand, how about yours?'

'Oh, I don't bother about that sort of thing,' I lie airily.

Untrue, untrue. You should see me addressing birthday cards from my son. Carefully putting the pen in my left hand to write: 'Love from Felix', even putting the F in backwards to make the whole thing look more authentic.

'Parents,' said Anthony Powell, 'are sometimes a bit of a disappointment to their children. They seldom fulfil the promises of their early years.'

I would like to be a devoted mother . . . but I do like a bit of peace sometimes . . . at least I think I do. A girlfriend has taken the children out for the day so I can work. My husband and the dog have gone to play cricket, and the house seems strangely quiet and empty. I must say I miss them all dreadfully . . .

Going to the Dogs

Much of my childhood was spent hawking our long-suffering golden retriever round local dog shows. He never won, except fourth prize once when there were only four dogs in the class, and he loathed every minute of it. To avenge himself, he invariably escaped during the show and had to be paged over the loudspeaker. 'Will the owner of Dog No.. . . currently demolishing the Fancy Gâteaux Stall . . .' It was with nostalgia, therefore, that I visited Crufts last week.

A smell of hot dog and hair lacquer hung on the foetid Olympia air. Everywhere there were rows of dogs on benches, sleeping, yawning, looking wistful, sprawled on fur rugs or candlewick counterpanes. Frenzied grooming was going on. If you have hairs to shed, prepare to shed them now.

In one corner there were briards – French Dougal dogs – all bouncing and peering through fringed curtains of hair. In another, Cavalier spaniels lay exquisitely beautiful in liquid heaps. In another, chows with black tongues and hangover frowns looked as though they had been at the red wine last night. Great Danes stood gentle and faintly apologetic like very tall girls at cocktail parties.

'How many dogs have you got, now, Lilian?'

'Oh, we're down to fifteen at the moment.'

The exhibitors were even more remarkable than their dogs. They fell into two distinct types: public-bar men with short Brylcreemed hair parted in the middle, very red necks, tattooed arms and fake sheepskin coats; and grizzled middle-class ladies with cropped hair, red veins, gin-soaked voices, cigarettes slotted into their lower lips and massive trousered bottoms.

A Doberman class was in progress. A great deal of doggery pokery going on. Even during the judging, exhibitors could not stop fiddling with their dogs, pulling out their legs, tugging them off the ground by non-existent tails, snapping fingers, brandishing hairbrushes and cloths to catch any trace of slobber. It was all very uncool – rather like lipsticking in public.

The fun really began when the dogs had to show off their paces, and each elephantine lady owner ran round the ring, pearls bouncing and falling on her vast twin-setted bosom.

The judges, clad in a little brief authority and tweed skirts, came straight out of the staffroom, as they stumped briskly round the ring, squatting down to look at the exhibits like golfers examining the lie of a putt.

The best five dogs were lined up nose to tail. Second was moved up to first place. Prizes were handed out. Firm handshakes exchanged. Dog number three, with understandable irritation, lost his temper and bit the winner. Fur and expletives were soon flying, dogs and cameramen snapping, as the two owners tore their dogs apart.

'Oh, please,' cried a girl reporter, scribbling frantically, 'would you mind repeating the last sentence?'

They did – and she turned very pink.

At the edge of the ring, a lady in a pork-pie hat brandished a bulldog-clipped petition. 'Exhibitors in favour of the retaining of docking, please sign here,' she said in a ringing voice.

Obedience classes were also in progress. Owners striding briskly up and down, like bowlers pacing out their runs, dogs following their owners like shadows, anxious eyes trying to read their minds. An Alsatian sat by itself in the ring for ten minutes – one of the tests – trembling with nerves, and licking its lips like a starlet interviewed on telly.

Around the hall were stalls with very smooth men flogging dog products: clipping devices, high-protein low-calorie dog biscuits, vaginal deodorants for bitches, Mr Groom – they have such absurd names. I always feel an idiot in the local grocer's asking for four large Pals, and two small Chums.

Do people really grow to look like their dogs? Certainly people who own the same breed tend to look like each other. The poodle ladies, for example, were very done up with lots of turquoise eyeshadow, white boots, spangles in their spun-glass hair, and cupid's-bow mouths bearing no relation to the thinness of their lips. But over on the Alsatian benches, it was all whine, women and throng, tough ladies in leather with very dyed black hair, who looked as though they spent their time writing letters to *Forum* on the delights of corporal punishment. Next door, the Great Danes seemed mostly to be manned by tweedy women with continental-shelf bosoms.

It was lunchtime. The Brylcreem brigade ate Spam and beetroot sandwiches. The large grizzled ladies tucked into pork pies, washed down with large nips of gin. I suppose if you're disappointed in men you turn to dogs, who give you uncritical adoration whether your hips spread or not.

A little girl slept leaning against a sleeping mastiff, a copy of *Squirrel Nutkin* lying open in her hands. Several dogs were covered in netting like raspberries to ward off the public.

'By the end of the day,' explained an owner, 'the dogs have got flat heads from patting. Some dogs take to it, some don't.'

The heat was becoming too much for the St Bernards. One got bored and launched himself off his bench like a great liner going into the water. It took three people to heave him back again. He had a flowered towel tied like a bib under his chin to stop him drooling.

'Quick, the graduate bitches are going into the ring.' I never knew dogs got degrees. B.Litters, I suppose.

Toys were upstairs, rather like Boots the Chemist. Here tweeness reigned supreme, every toy dog sitting in a cage hung with curtains in tartan, flowered chintz or velvet.

'My doggy loves to be surrounded by beauty,' said a Peke owner, giving the dog little bits of turkey with fat heavily ringed fingers.

I left suffering from a fit of Peke.

Downstairs, delicious Pyrenean mountain dogs shuffled round like animated fur rugs. One edged towards a row of picnicking teenagers and slyly helped himself to a sandwich. With total disregard to Crufts Rule 28 about no bitches being mated on the precincts, one dog climbed laboriously on top of another.

Yet I must confess, as a biased setter owner, that I found most delectable of all the rows of English setters – lovely freckled heads lolling, plumed tails swinging, Groucho Marx eyebrows shooting up and down. Once in the ring they turned it into a great cock-leg party: snuffling, goosing, gambolling, beseeching the judge to join in their silly setter games.

But as I left I wondered how much the dogs really enjoy the palaver. A friend who exhibits her dog regularly said that recently before a show she bathed him in scented soap. Afterwards he gave her the slip. She found him at the bottom of the garden, digging frenziedly, dirtying himself up. When she looked to see what he was burying – it was the scented soap.

Carols

I love carols – they have the same shining innocence and lack of pretension as medieval frescoes. And one of my favourite pastimes is browsing and playing my way through the *Oxford Book of Carols*. From the first page one is drawn into a magic world – a sort of Monteverdi's Flying Circus – full of obscure medieval songs about cuckoos, genuflecting cherry trees, Fillpale the cow, and the Girt Dog of Langport who burnt his long tail.

Even characters as exotic as the Magi take on a cheerful homespun quality:

> *Three kings are here both wealthy and wise,*
> *Come riding far o'er the snow-covered ice.*
> *The search for the Child, the redeemer of wrong*
> *With tambours and drums, they go sounding along.*

Unlike hymn, the word 'carol' is of a dancing origin, and meant to dance in a ring, which I suppose accounts for their joyous lilting quality:

> *Joseph did whistle and Mary did sing,*
> *On Christmas Day, on Christmas Day,*
> *And all the bells on earth did ring.*

I love all the domestic touches. Mary having a pregnant woman's craving for cherries, and Joseph snapping back with understandable asperity.

'Let him pluck thee a cherry that brought thee now with child.'

I often wonder how seriously the Middle Ages took the virgin birth. They're always making sly cracks about Joseph being an old man, an old man was he.

The footnotes in the *Oxford Book* are absolute bliss. 'We regret,' writes the editor about the laxness of one parish church, 'that A Virgin Unspotted has been dropped at Grasmere.' One has visions of her coming down by parachute. And I never knew the comma in 'God Rest Ye Merry, Gentlemen' came after the word Merry, or that Mendelssohn wrote the music for 'Hark the Herald Angels'.

Then there are the verses of carols starred as being too secular to be sung in church:

> *Call up the Butler of this house*
> *Put on his golden ring.*
> *Let him bring us a glass of beer,*
> *And the better we shall sing.*

I love the titles to the tunes: Old Winchester, Bristol, St George, Maidstone and Sidney – they sound like cruisers or brands of sherry; and some of the authors are rather bizarre. Half the earlier carols seem to have been taken from the Latin of C. Coffin. Or written by Bishop Woodford and Compilers (which sounds more like a pop group). And typically it's only in a French carol that Mary keeps harping on about missing dinner, when poor Joseph is desperately searching for an inn.

'Good King Wenceslas' is wildly topical at the moment with everyone rushing round the petrol pumps gathering winter fuel. We were always ticked off at school for whooping when we sang the word 'Fu-oo-el'.

The author of 'Good King W.', who was called John Mason Neale (we had a good laugh over that at school), gets an absolute pasting in the *Oxford Book*. The editors describe the carol as 'doggerel, poor and commonplace to the last degree, owing its popularity to the delightful tune'.

I must confess a rather soft spot for 'Good King W.' Admittedly it does end in mid-air. We never discover if the King and his deep-frozen page ever reach Yonder Peasant. I suspect they got fed up with trailing through the snow, and drank all the wine, ate all the flesh to keep themselves warm – a sort of wassail-stop tour. History doesn't relate what they did with the pine logs.

People seem to forget there are carols for all seasons of the year, whenever there's occasion for rejoicing. I think spring and summer carols have the same exotic out-of-season glamour of autumn crocuses and Christmas roses.

John Mason Neale apart, the Victorians committed some terrible crimes in the name of carols. Mrs Alexander rabbiting on in 'Once in Royal David's City' about tears and smiles. Christina Rossetti's fearful dirge about the bleak midwinter: 'Snow had fallen, snow on snow, snow on snow.' She probably couldn't think what to put. She was also inaccurate. It doesn't snow in Bethlehem at Christmas. The temperature is normally around 57 degrees Fahrenheit, and, says the Meteorological Office, it rains more than it does in London in December.

On the other hand, many of the twentieth-century writers recaptured the beauty and simplicity of medieval carols. Take one by Chesterton:

The Christchild stood at Mary's knee
And all his hair was like a crown
And all the flowers looked up at him
And all the stars looked down.

In the *Oxford Book*, learned doctors are always being woken at six o'clock on Christmas morning by the sweet singing of mill girls. I wish Putney carol singers would take a leaf out of their book. From mid-November we get bombarded by teenagers ringing our bell to the accompaniment of stifled giggles croaking out, 'We wish you a merry Christmas,' and then forgetting the words.

I'm not very keen either on those organised parties of carol singers: asexual briskies; high-complexioned ladies tossing their heads in time to the music; tenors in spectacles with drips on the ends of their noses.

But then I'm always embarrassed when people sing at me personally. Not that it stopped me carol singing as a child, hawking my Barnardo's box with the hole in the bottom round the local gentry, failing miserably to reach those top Es in 'Hark the Herald Angels'.

I'm sure people gave me money to go away.

One Christmas I was even selected to play the carols for house prayers at school. Alas, I was rather smug about it beforehand, which drove an iconoclastic friend to put Bronco (a now discontinued stiff and shiny lavatory paper) inside the piano against the strings. As a result, 'Little Town of Bethlehem' came out as a sort of Honky Tonk Pizzicato. I got so flustered I missed the repeat sign in the first verse and stumbled through the whole carol two lines ahead of the choir. Fortunately our housemistress was tone-deaf.

We enjoyed carols at school. Once we started singing them, it meant the end of term was near and there were all those frightful schoolgirl jokes about shepherds washing their socks by night, and the Angel Gabriel ringing for womb service. Today my two-year-old daughter is merrily carrying on the tradition:

> *Goosey, Goosey Gander*
> *Upstairs downstairs,*
> *In my lady's manger.*

But I think what ultimately enchants one about carols – 'those masterpieces of tantalising simplicity' – is their gaiety and grace:

> *The rising of the sun*
> *The running of the deer*
> *The playing of the merry organ*
> *Sweet singing in the choir*

They seem to call to us from a less complex world, where people were happier, less materialistic, and delighted in making their own music together, instead of having their minds blown by a pounding of gramophones, wireless and television.

As the writer of the introduction to the *Oxford Book* pointed out in 1928: 'It should be possible to restore such spontaneous and imperishable things to general use. . . perhaps, nothing is just now of such importance as to increase the element of joy in religion.'

Today, he might have added the words 'and in life' as well. Carols seem to challenge us to be merrier, love and joy come to you.*

* I was so delighted that the great conductor André Previn wrote me a fan letter after this piece.

Paws

The queues for *Jaws* are so long at the local cinema, it's impossible to get a seat. But this hardly matters when we've a perfectly good *Jaws* drama raging in Putney – with me, alas, cast in the unenviable role of the Shark's mistress.

It began last March when we acquired a second dog, a tight-skinned, curly-tailed mongrel, whom we called Fortnum and who was suffering from a deprived childhood. As a puppy he was found hanging by wire from a stone cross in a nearby graveyard. After being cut down, he was given to a family who decided a few weeks later that a dog was too much of a nuisance. I met him on the way to the Battersea Dogs Home, and, always a sucker for a sob story, took him home with me.

He has rewarded his reprieve with touching gratitude, following me around like a shadow. His merriness and charm are belied only by his eyes, which have the marmoset sadness of the death cell, and by his desperate insecurity, which makes him howl whenever I go out.

Recently, however, this insecurity took on a more sinister form. Accustomed to roughhousing with the Senior Dog, who takes punishment like a punchbag, Fortnum has started getting stroppy on the Common, charging up to other dogs and, when they won't romp with him, snapping his ivory teeth like a shark and picking a fight.

Even worse, he enlists the aid of the Senior Dog, who never started a fight in his life. Together they rampage around like licentious soldiery, displaying terriertorial imperative.

Such behaviour does not promote serenity in one's life. My lovely Common, which in the old days was such a refuge from the pressures of life, has become a nightmare. Gone are the days of peaceful ramblings, watching the squirrels swing in the holly trees, considering every flower that grows. I am far too busy now, charging about with my new-cut ash stick, separating brawlers, or peering through the tombstones for approaching dog walkers.

In the good old days, I used to edge clear of people who walked the Common without a dog, in case they were flashers or worse. Now that seems like a day at the country compared with the venom of the blue-rinsed old bags at

the end of furiously yapping, red-ribboned Yorkshire terriers. I dread going out. I am suffering from Old
Bagrophobia.

Matters reached a head three weeks ago, when I walked
the dogs later than usual, and the Common was crawling
with exhausted mothers trailing fractious children and
depressed-looking King Charles spaniels. Suddenly the Senior Dog, who is notorious for the ambiguity of his libido,
sighted the love of his life, a castrated male golden retriever,
and, hurtling across the Common, leapt lustily upon him to
the hysterical screams of the retriever's owner.

Next moment Fortnum rolled up, yapping encouragement
and waving an old French letter he'd found in the church-
yard. Then out of the corner of his eye, he spied an old enemy,
a Border terrier. Hackles rose on both sides. Next moment,
the fur was flying.

I was whimpering apologies, desperately trying to separate
fornicators and fighters, when a lady with an iron-grey bun
rose out of the oak saplings, fierce as ten furies, terrible
as hell.

'Your dogs are the scourge of Putney,' she bellowed in a
deep baritone. 'You're a disgrace to the neighbourhood. I
know you, Jilly. I am Mrs Nicholas Simpson.'

It was the final straw. I went off next day and bought Fortnum a muzzle, but he looked so pathetic in it, like a flowerpot in one of those white plastic containers, that I hadn't the heart to make him wear it.

I looked for help in books on psychiatric disturbance: Doctor Spock, Lorenz on Aggression, The Wolfman and Sigmund Freud. All stressed that punishment was the least desirable method of controlling aggression, but children who have feelings of insecurity engaged more in harassment of others than well-adjusted children.

'He's got to be made more secure at home,' I told my husband, who was bawling Fortnum out for goosing the cat. 'I always said he should be tied up,' he said.

Another textbook claimed that the answer to overtly aggressive groups was not social interaction, but to unite them against a common problem, and explained how two rival gangs became the best of friends, after spending an afternoon locating a leak in a gas pipe. I can't really see myself rallying Fortnum and the Senior Dog, and a lot of cairns and Yorkshire terriers into looking for leaks. They're too busy having them.

In some ways things are improving. As a result of vigilance and stick brandishing, Fortnum hasn't had a fight for nearly three weeks, but his reputation as the Jaws of Putney has spread like wildfire.

I have only to set foot on the Common now for people I've never seen before to rush up and tell me to put my bloody dog on a lead. At my approach, old ladies leap for the thickets, Pomeranians are thrust into the protection of briar patches like Brer Rabbit, mothers run screaming to the Common Ranger, cabals gather in corners, shaking fists and muttering.

The whole thing has become a witch-hunt. Fear, as Froude said, is the parent of cruelty. No doubt the poor old ladies have nightmares about Fortnum swimming through the long blond grass, ivory jaws snapping, hell-bent on disembowelling their darlings, so they retaliate by hurling abuse at me next morning.

Perhaps the dogs and I should live in the country in a little cottage with neuroses growing over the door. Perhaps I should take my husband on a lead next time to intimidate the old bags, or be more positive and rise out of the oak saplings first, bellowing: 'Take your terrier off my mongrel, I am Mrs Leo Cooper.'

I suppose it's all experience. I now know exactly what it feels like to be Crippen's mother (he was always a good boy to me, M'lord). At the moment Jaws of Putney sits on my knee, being typed around, bristling out of the window at two passing cairns (dreaming no doubt of Chihuahua on Toast or Peke Vol-au-Vent). In a minute I shall have to run the gauntlet of the Common again. Thank God he's not a bitch, or in the current mood we might easily get a Killing of Sister Jaws.

At Lord's

Now that the captains and wicketkeepers have departed, and the battle's tumult has moved to White Hart Lane, now that the bells have tolled the knell of parting Ray . . . I would like to tell you of two days I spent at the Lord's Test last week watching England playing the West Indies.

The first thing I noticed on arrival at the ground was a large stand saying 'Rovers Only'. I imagined a great crowd of dogs inside, all barking, slobbering over one another and generally creating chaos.

The second thing that struck me was hordes of glamorous men looking all beamish and excited to be there, clutching *The Times* and their first surreptitious glass of beer. *Quelle richesse*, I thought – but I was wrong. Men watching cricket aren't interested in girls. There is something about going through a turnstile that seems to de-sex the male, a kind of symbolic emasculation.

The Lord's Test is in fact a great misogynists' jamboree, where men revert to their schooldays, when girls were soppy dates. Wandering round on my own, I felt as though I'd strayed into the Athenaeum or a Gents.

Lord's is also a gluttons' High Noon. Fellow spectators never stopped eating and drinking. All round me, they rushed back and forth, slopping four pints of beer at a time, smacking their lips as they unpacked vast hampers, choking on Scotch eggs, guzzling and swilling and stuffing themselves with pork pies, cream cakes and buns.

'Being out of doors makes one so hungry,' said a plump girl as she embarked on her fifth cheese roll.

I was also disturbed catching glimpses of long golden manes trailing down bare suntanned backs and thinking, Yow! Naked girls! What is Lord's coming to? Then the back would turn round and I'd be confronted with a beard or a large hairy arm reaching for the Party Seven.

On my left was an eager pink-faced girl and her fiancé, who was wearing a Free Foresters tie. He was initiating her into the mysteries of the game.

'Well, first that chap bowls six balls, then another chap bowls six.'

'Why six?' she said fondly.

'Well, six is a useful sort of number,' he said patiently.

'Get out while you can,' I wanted to shout at her, 'you don't know the hours of spreading sandwiches and getting grass stains off flannels that await you.'

There was so much going on off the field that one was almost able to forget the cricket. I tried to watch, but it was very dull. The West Indies had scored eighty-seven, when England got a second wicket, and everyone perked up, like that moment in a pub when you've all been clutching empty glasses for ages, and someone suddenly offers to buy a round of drinks.

Lunch and the gluttons all trotted off to buy more food. While queuing half an hour for a sandwich I marvelled at the élan of the West Indian spectators as they paraded up and down, so tall and princely with their flashing jewellery and their coloured suits – turning Lord's into a male Ascot.

Lunch over, and West Indian star Kanhai batted on and on. The gluttons were still guzzling; the choc bar consumption had reached pyrotechnic heights. The beer intake was hotting up, too – almost a can a minute when Ray Illingworth came on to bowl.

The eager pink-faced girl was now wilting in the face of a barrage of information from her fiancé:

'Now that was an off break. Watch carefully, he may do it again.'

'Why are they clapping now?'

'Because he's putting his sweater on.'

The poor girl looked utterly bemused.

'What do you think of the game?' asked her fiancé.

'Oh, lovely,' she said faintly. 'But they're such a long way away. I can't see their faces.'

'Watch their feet, that's far more interesting.'

In fact the part of the players' anatomy one is most conscious of is their bottoms, whether they're running up to bowl, bending in the slips, or standing with their backs to you in the deep. I kept myself awake deciding which player had the most boring bottom. In the end Underwood and Arnold tied for first place.

Kanhai got his hundred, the West Indians exploded in jubilation. T-shirts were covered in beer stains, children balanced along the boundary rails.

I spent hours tracking down a loo. Lord's typically was swarming with Gents, but not with Ladies. Once there, I heard a great roar of applause, a wicket had fallen. It's just as my husband says, you only have to go for a pee and something exciting happens, so you have to rush back, zipping up your trousers, to find you've missed a hat trick. I am told the illustrious Warner Stand has slits cut in the loo walls so you needn't miss a ball.

Geoffrey Boycott, another star from Yorkshire, was fielding nearby, and his fan club much in evidence, cheering him every time he put a finger to the ball. What a strange tense creature he is, with his collar turned up against some imagined storm, his sleeves rolled down and left unbuttoned, and his cap with the long beak-like peak like Ducky Daddies in my son's Henny Penny story.

On the second day, as West Indian spirits soared, the English crowd seemed to surrender and abandon themselves to the sheer voluptuous pleasure of watching great cricket. It was as though Sobers and Julien had assumed a divinity, and we were witnessing not just a contest between England and the West Indies, but between men and gods.

Halfway through the morning Fletcher dropped a catch, and suddenly the whole ground was hissing with speculation, as though onions had been tossed into a pan of boiling fat. The Boycott Fan Club grew more and more clamorous.

'Put Boycott on to bowl.'

'Come on, Sir Geoff-free, when's the Queen goin' to recognise you?'

Boycott gave them a pussycat smirk.

Fifties came and went. Poor bowlers – all that pounding and windmilling to no avail. Poor Illingworth seemed to have aged ten years in two days.

In front of me, a glutton ate a whole ginger cake and then a Swiss roll, straight down, peeling off the paper like a choc bar, but in an abstracted way, as though he was only eating to stem his misery. I didn't blame him. I've always thought the only thing that makes cricket bearable is to be backing the winning side.

But suddenly there was a bonus. Greig was sent to field in the deep, just in front of me, and goodness what a beauty he is, tall and golden as a sunflower, with massive shoulders and long legs! Cricket has found an answer to David Duckham at last. And I wouldn't mind making Hayes while the sun shines either.

Poor Greig misfielded a ball and returned to the boundary to consistent barracking.

'The summer's running out for you, Phyllis,' shouted a wag.

'Why are they all so vile to him?' I asked.

'He's too good-looking and too useless to have crowd appeal,' said my neighbour. 'Oh, shot, sir, shot, what a lovely shot!'

Finally Kanhai put England out of their misery and declared. England came out to bat, and calypso was followed by collapso, to the extremely irritating ecstasy of the West Indians. The Battle of Kanhai had become a slaughter.

As I was leaving, I bumped into the pink-faced girl and her Free Foresters fiancé. She looked as if she were sleep-walking.

'Don't worry,' he was saying briskly, 'you'll get the hang of it by the fifth day.'

On Friendship

When a second *Sunday Times* series on the Pleasures of Life was suggested, Sex, Food and Drink were bandied about as possible subjects. As I try out anything I write, I thought I had better keep off sex, for obvious reasons – and food as well, or I would put on a stone, or drink, or I would end up a sozzled heap in the gutter. So I chose friendship, which seemed a safe enough subject but had equally dire consequences. In order to study my friends, I filled the house with them for two months, and nearly lost the best friend I've got – my husband.

We are now reeling from crony fatigue – all passion and next month's salary spent. You have only to look at our drink bill to realise that whoever said: 'If you've got friends and neighbours, you're the richest guy in town,' needed his head examining.

To be appreciated, friends should be enjoyed like wine, in moderation. A few years ago, I was shocked to hear that a very distinguished art historian, when asked to meet Georges Braque, had written back: 'Sir X and Lady X thank the Directors of the Tate Gallery very much for their kind invitation to meet Georges Braque but regret that they already have enough friends.'

Today, I understand Sir X exactly. I don't have enough time to see the people I love. As I flip through old address books and Christmas cards and six years of postcards collected in the toast rack, I am appallingly aware of the friends who have flowed through my life and been lost, because I never wrote or rang back, or didn't feel sure enough of my cooking to ask them back to dinner.

Fortunately, many of one's lost friends turn up again. Some you can pick up after ten years like favourite books, and they're just as beguiling – others date. One misconception about friendship is that there's something wrong with you if you can't sustain a relationship over thirty years. People change, and just because one shared a crush on Rock Hudson in the fifties, it doesn't mean one has anything in common today.

At typing school in Oxford, I was taken in like a stray kitten by a school friend's parents. In the end I became more a friend of theirs than her. He was a vicar, she a classics don

related to Lewis Carroll. She had a slow sing-song Blooms-
bury voice, looked like Edith Evans, and crouched by the gas
fire deliberately burning toast because she liked it that way.
Intellectuals wandered in and out, and I listened enchanted
as their conversation flowed forth like a jewelled river. One
day she handed me a book. 'Have you read it? You'll enjoy it.'

It was the Rieu translation of the *Odyssey*. I took it to bed
and read it like a novel in one sitting. Under her guidance, I
followed Sophocles, Euripides, Sappho, Aeschylus. Often she
read from the Greek Epigrams. I can still remember the sing-
song voice, the hissing fire, the smell of burning toast:

'Constantia, inconstant one, I heard thy name and thought
it beautiful, but thou art to me, more bitter than death, thou
fliest him, who lovest thee, and him who lovest thee not thou
pursuest, that he may love thee, and thou mayest fly him
again.'

That epigram seemed to sum up the whole transient, heart-
breaking world of husband-hunting on which I was about to
embark. From Oxford I went to London to share a flat with
two other girls, an air hostess who looked like a gazelle and
used to smuggle miniature brandy bottles in her bra, and a
larky ex-deb, who arrived from Devon on Sundays with
clotted cream and flowers from Daddy's herbaceous border,

and vigorously scrubbed the kitchen floor to Brahms's *Academic Festival Overture*.

Girls looking for husbands are not unlike foxhounds too interested in the quarry to relate much to outside influences. My two stable or unstable mates were all I needed in the way of female friendship. I adored the endless speculation, the unstoppered scent bottles, wearing each other's clothes, playing Frank Sinatra and Ella Fitzgerald fortissimo, going off all tarted up to parties, and shrieking about our exploits when we returned at three o'clock in the morning.

United in spiky competition, we were deeply critical of each other's men. It became almost more important that a boyfriend should impress the rest of the flat than he should please you. Whenever you tried to smuggle a new man in, the other two invariably emerged from the kitchen, cheeks bulging with scrambled egg, or dripping from the bath or even in rollers to have a look. If they didn't approve, they would disappear into the bathroom, and mutter like witches – and another romance would bite the dust – admittedly, in our flat there was plenty of dust to bite.

Then finally, with a sigh of relief, came marriage – the quarry landed, one's attitude to friendship had to change. One was no longer a rackety wench, but half of 'the Coopers',

'an awfully sweet couple', and socially a much more accept-
able proposition. It was a bit of a shock for me to discover one
couldn't have men friends in the same gloriously abandoned
way, or girl friends either.

Being a forceful character, my husband made short work
of any of my friends he considered boring or unstable. He
couldn't bear all the chatter about clogged pores. As my
father once said to my mother: 'I've nothing against other
women, darling, except they make you so boring.'

But there were ample compensations. Some of the happiest moments in my life have been waiting for a party to
begin, painting my face upstairs, as Handel organ concertos
thundered through the house to the accompaniment of popping corks as my husband opened crates of cheap plonk to
'let it breathe'. Then friends arriving, the endless chatter and
laughter, and later sorties to the fish and chip shop or the
Chinese takeaway so the night could be extended intermin-
ably. Or later, when we moved to Putney, similar evenings in
the garden, with the scent of the tobacco plants and the white
roses luminous in the dusk, all mirth and merriment until
the stars came out to join us.

With marriage one also came up forcefully against men's
friendship with other men, those all-male evenings out on

the toot, egging each other on, ringing up each other's wives to say that they'll be late. I am always reminded of Chippy Hackee and Timmy Tiptoes stuck down a tree trunk, stuffing themselves with nuts, singing in thin and fat squirrel voices, and refusing to come home.

The way men feel mentally uncorseted with men is also marvellously illustrated in *Anna Karenina*, when Vronsky, enjoying himself with friends at a post-election party, suddenly receives a telegram from Anna telling him their child is sick and he must come home: 'Vronsky was suddenly struck by the contrast of the innocent festivities over the election and the sombre burdensome love to which he must return.'

Through marriage, I witnessed all too often the 'innocent festivities' of the rugger world, where the men expected the same camaraderie *they* achieved by wallowing in the mud, jumping about naked together in a hot plunge bath, and drinking pints of beer afterwards, to be also achieved by their wives as they sourly scraped paste on to a piece of bread on to which someone had already scraped margarine.

Unable to discuss deep freezes, incapable of running up a jam roll, I failed to establish a rapport with many of the other rugger wives, but it was during one of these spreading sessions that I met one of my dearest friends. She was brought along by one of the forwards, and refused to do any spreading at all. An inconstant nymph with vast aquamarine eyes, at only eighteen she had achieved the sort of career, as Nicolas Bentley once said, that made the Recording Angel think seriously about taking up shorthand. Wherever she went, she generated excitement. Seeing her even today instantly evokes those obsessive, uneasy, sex-surfeited days when I was first married.

As I've always enjoyed the role of friend as dustbin, I was very happy to down tools and listen every time she turned up to 'boast or complain' about the latest saga in her love life. One of her charms, apart from making one feel the one person in the world she wanted to see, was her lack of moderation. Once in a restaurant she ordered a carafe of whisky and drank the lot. All the waiters lined up and shook hands with her as she walked out. Another time she ate a whole pint of Devonshire cream with her finger between Tiverton and Ilchester.

When we moved to Fulham she followed, coming for a night and staying for two years, house guestating, a constant delight. One winter she developed a cough and, having lost the cork of her cough mixture, decanted it into a whisky bottle and while travelling to work used to take great swigs, to the fascinated horror of the entire 30 bus. Fairly soon her boy-friend, who was in the middle of a divorce, was spending odd nights with us too. At dawn when I had to get up to feed the baby, and groped my way groggily downstairs, my fingers would encounter his fur coat hung over the banister, and I would think: 'Oh, good, full house again.' He used to get up shortly after me. 'Can't you stay longer?' I once heard her grumbling. 'I can't, darling, don't you see, I've got to get home, get undressed and into bed before the children and the *au pair* come in to wake me.'

Shortly afterwards the ceiling gave way under them.

One of the great fascinations of friendship is introducing friends to friends, and seeing how they get on. Often it doesn't work, because each one is used to the searchlight beam of your attention and bitterly resents its being turned on to some-one else. Also, if you have a chameleon character, you behave differently with different people, jolly joke-cracking clown with one, marvelling sycophant with another, and have great difficulty when they meet in reconciling the roles.

I have always thought it would be a cruel but interesting journalistic exercise to ask Person X to write down her ten best friends, then ask the ten to name their own ten best and see how many of them selected X. How embarrassing if none of them did. And if one made one's own list, could one actually get up to ten? How many men would one dare include – in case they thought you were being forward, or their wives or girlfriends became jealous, particularly if you hadn't included them as well.

Friendship with the opposite sex is a complex matter. Is it ever entirely platonic? Sometimes one has good relationships with old boyfriends, but so often they never get off the ground because the old flames feel guilty about ditching you, or vice versa. Perhaps the best friendships are with men where the relationship has never been consummated, kept on slow burn, sort of Grecian Earnests, for-ever-will-he-love-you-be-fair. But even in a sexual relationship, the gossiping and the companionship are all-important; sex is only the liquid centre of the great Newberry Fruit of friendship.

Since I stopped working in an office, I do miss male company. You can get so close to people you work with, laying ambushes for the office crone, speculating about the typing pool's love life, that when you leave you vow to meet every week for lunch. But you find as the weeks pass that you have less and less in common; the atrocities of the office crone, or the way Gloria flashed her thighs at the managing director, seem less and less interesting. Once a week becomes once a month; like a wireless battery running down, a surge of chat followed by longer and longer silences, until the whole thing peters out altogether.

I've long been fascinated, too, by the love-hate element in friendship. Harvey Smith is David Broome's best friend, but he is also the person it gives him most satisfaction to beat. And I am sure Coleridge wasn't all that distressed when Wordsworth got a bad review. Certainly another of Wordsworth's friends, De Quincey, wrote with positive relish about the awfulness of Wordsworth's legs: 'It was really a pity, as I agreed with a lady in thinking, that he had not another pair of legs for evening dress – when no boots lend their friendly aid to mask our imperfections.'

'In the misfortunes of our best friends,' wrote La Rochefoucauld, 'there is something not unpleasing,' to be echoed three centuries later by Violet Elizabeth Bott: 'She's my best friend, I hate her.'

I certainly feel a stronger stab of jealousy if one of my friends lands a delectable man, or her child wins a scholarship to Winchester, than I do if it happens to an enemy. Generally, though, if one's friends do achieve something marvellous, after the initial envious stab, one passes through the jealousy barrier to bask in their reflected glory. One of my great friends, Philippa Pullar, lives in Putney, and it was with real excitement recently that I received a copy of her biography of Frank Harris. Since it arrived, I have been brandishing its solid achievement in front of everyone who comes to the house.

'Seen Philippa's book? She's a *great* friend of ours,' and, particularly if there's another lady writer about who might be jealous: 'She's had absolutely *wonderful* reviews.'

Philippa also has very nice children – one of the compensations of growing old is flirting with one's friend's offspring – I quite fancy myself as 'close bosom friend of the maturing son'.

Traditionally, chiding one's friends into better behaviour, the mutual exchange of home truths, is supposed to be a vital element in friendship. I can do without it myself. I don't enjoy people telling me my dogs or children are out of control, or as a friend said the other day: 'I think you'd make a better wife if you brushed your hair and cooked more.' The friend's role is to admire, sympathise and amuse. As Dame Rebecca West said at a party the other day: 'I want to be a piece of asparagus with melted butter poured permanently over me.'

I fulfilled that ambition recently when one of our very best friends moved next door to us. It might have been tricky, but we'd already survived the baptism fire of two holidays together, when everyone but us swapped partners and left the stage strewn with corpses.

From such disaster, a great friendship was formed. Now, when I feel in need of cheer, I potter next door for a large drink and a metaphorical dock leaf to soothe away the nettle stings of the day. Our relationship is fairly sophisticated: we swap bottles of gin, garlic and gerbils, but seldom cups of sugar. Occasionally we borrow each other's records, a case of 'I scratch your Bach if you scratch mine.'

But finally, I suppose one of the greatest pleasures of friendship comes from the laughs. 'Why do we live,' said Mr Bennet, 'but to make sport for our neighbours and laugh at them in our turn.'

Half the fun if they behave badly is the indignation meetings – Watts-Dunton summoning his friends to discuss what to do 'for and about Swinburne'.

Recently my husband had a cataclysmic squawking match with one of our friends locally. As I was the cause of it, I tried to keep a low profile for the next week. Alas, our flaming great dog kept escaping and racing past her house, and I, to the glee of all our other neighbours, had to crawl past to get him each time on my hands and knees in case she saw me over the fence.

And so it goes on. People slip into one's life, stay for a while, casting a spell, or shedding innocence, then fall back into their own biographies, combining in a group, or giving way to one another with criss-cross and bewildering alternation. What became of Waring since he gave us all the slip?

Recently I was bewailing the five-year disappearance of one of my husband's oldest friends since he'd gone to live in darkest Kent. Then the other night our nanny's best friend, having been slung rather ignominiously out of her job, was taking refuge on the sofa in our drawing room.

Imagine her terror at two o'clock in the morning when the window flew up, the curtains parted, and climbing gingerly through came a man in spectacles wearing a bowler hat, and carrying a briefcase and a long umbrella.

'Who the hell do you think you are?' she gasped. To which he replied: 'I am one of Leo Cooper's oldest friends.'

Middle Age

'We want you to write about the Middle Age Crisis.'

I winced. It's all right for *me* to admit I'm middle-aged, so that everyone can hotly deny it, but it's not so jolly coming from someone else. Though God knows who I'm kidding, the signs of decay are already in evidence: ostrich feet round the eyes, crêpe on the thigh. Changing my parting last week, I even discovered my first grey hair. Praying it might have been bleached by the sun, I examined it more closely and found two more – all definitely grey. Parting is all we need of hell.

Hands give you away, say the women's mags. About once a month I remember to slap some Nulon on, but always put on too much, and have to wipe it off on the dogs. They're looking very young at the moment. I think I really admitted I was getting old last summer when I put moisturiser on my neck for the first time.

The Middle Age Crisis boils down to whether one will be able to attract men any more. Will the change of life mean a change of wife? Not that I want hordes of men after me, but I do like to keep my options open. I'd like to feel I could still rustle up the odd admirer in retaliation if my husband suddenly developed a mad passion for his secretary. I don't want to go to orgies either, but I don't want to get too wrinkled and repulsive to be asked.

'I reckon we've got about ten years' pulling power,' I said to my best friend the other day. Then I remembered I'd said exactly the same thing when I was eighteen, and when I was twenty-eight. No doubt I'll be still saying it in my nineties. Middle age, says Chambers, with uncharacteristic slyness, 'is an area between youth and age, usually reckoned to suit the reckoner'.

Pulling power, of course, depends a lot on clothes, but while I want to dress sexily, I shrink from being mutton dressed as lamb. I noticed some country wives looking very askance at my see-through sweater the other night, and at the other end of the scale, my son has got very disapproving recently and keeps buttoning up my shirt before I go out, in case 'anyone sees anything'.

So this is to be my future. Farewell plunge and cleavage, hail tunic tops, wool shirtwaisters to flatter the pear-shaped figure, touches of white near the face, all-in-one corselettes and support hose.

And what the hell am I going to do about my hair? I really don't fancy a grey bun. When I was thirty-five, I vowed I'd cut my hair when I was forty, but now there are only two years to go, and Bardot hasn't cut hers yet. Perhaps I should have a fringe to make myself look younger, but it's so awful when the wind blows it sideways and you suddenly age ten years as a corrugated forehead is revealed.

The books on staying young are so dismal. They all tell you to give up booze and lying in the sun. I think that's junk, booze and sun make me jolly, and nothing ages one quicker than feeling miserable. They're always banging on, too, about the right diet and one's cholesterol level.

'You're trying to give me a heart attack,' grumbles my husband, pouring a sauce groaning with cream and wine over a second helping of chicken.

'Well, at least have one early,' I snap, 'so I'm young enough to get someone else.'

I was slightly startled when my doctor leaned across at a dinner party the other night and told me my husband would have to spend the rest of his life on Flora.

Middle age, however, is much less daunting if you've got a loving partner to grow old with. The owl and the pussycat went to seed in a beautiful pea-green boat. Having young children helps, too, because you can still kid yourself you're a young mum.

I have noticed an increasing restlessness in my forty-year-old girlfriends. Some start issuing marriage-or-nothing ultimatums to their lovers. Some, criticised constantly by teenage children and assailed by vague feelings that they haven't achieved very much in life, start taking degrees or going to evening classes. Others wonder very reluctantly if they ought to go back to work. Some have even started lying about their age, which is stupid, as people always find out and add at least ten years to your real age when they pass the story on. The worst-hit seem to be unhappily married women, who suddenly get a feeling of now or never – 'I've only got one life. Should I get out before it's too late, and gamble on finding someone else?'

Unfortunately the field narrows as one grows older. If a man in his forties wants to push off, there are scores of young girls slavering to snap him up, but society frowns on a woman who shacks up with younger men, particularly after the menopause, when she won't be able to give him any children.

I notice, too, the fatalism with which a woman expects her young lover to push off. What she doesn't realise is she won't lose him because she's older – no one looks at anyone they're married to after a few years anyway. It's the neuroticism, the feverish insecurity, the endless demands for reassurance, the jealousy, that drive him away.

What unnerves me about middle age is how to play it. On some days I see myself growing old disgracefully, blazing gloriously in the autumn of my life in leopard-skin coats with streaked hair and roulette chips rattling round in the bottom of my bag. Then I remember that character is supposed to show in the face after a certain age, so I try to be good for a day or two. Certainly the thought of the Change of Life puts the fear of God into me. The crow's feet are nothing to what will be unleashed according to that old misery guts Simone de Beauvoir:

'The menopausal woman,' she writes, 'is likely to become frigid or alternatively overwhelm her husband with her demands. Homosexual tendencies will become manifest, she may take up masturbation and seek romance she has never known, and soon will no longer be able to know.'

And as if that wasn't enough: 'She will also know a mad desire for prostitution. Her dreams will be peopled by erotic fantasies and she will fall in love with one young man after another.'

Oh dear, hot flushes and hot crushes. Will I find myself at fifty, bribing passing youths with mopeds?

Even more depressing are those awful remedies for keeping sex going – the utter dinginess of oestrogen pessaries for a dehydrated vagina. My doctor swears by implants. I'm not so sure – I'd rather have a him plant, and grow my own men. I'm sure I'd have more success than I did with courgettes last summer.

But how can one lessen the middle-aged crises? By devouring four romantic novels a week – philistine is supposed to fortify the over-forties. One should also have several friends who are still very glamorous but slightly older, to make one feel younger.

I'm encouraged by the fact that the rate I'm tottering down life's sunless hill, I may well get shot of the menopause before my daughter embarks on adolescence. And, as I wrote a vast cheque for a pair of trousers this week, I justified it to myself that one has to spend a bit more on one's clothes as one gets older.

And as I get older I get increasing pleasure not only from my family and friends, but from my books and garden, and

my dogs and cats, and from my lovely Common now turning golden outside. For Nature, as Wordsworth pointed out,
never betrays the heart that loves her.

I also have a suspicion that if a woman is jaunty and has a
gleam in the eye, she can go on having fun until she's a hundred, and that the menopause is but a short pause in
getting men.

Sold to the Blonde . . .

Crossing the threshold of Sotheby's, you feel the sacred fris-
son, that special reverence evoked by great art and vast sums
of money.

Polite young men directed me through warehouses
crammed with headless statues to a sale of 'rare wines'. It was
like being in church. Everyone whispered except the auctioneer, who addressed us in bell-like tones from a pulpit.
Handsome, drawn-faced, he had the grave courtesy of Plan-
tagenet Palliser. On closer inspection he turned out to be an
old flame of my sister-in-law. I resisted winking at him in
case he thought I was bidding.

'Here is a nice case of Moët et Chandon for your inexpen-
sive birthday party,' he said with a slight smile.

The audience shook with silent laughter, as the lot went for
£68. No one says 'going going gorn' any more, apparently,
because it takes up too much time. A jeroboam of Château

Mouton Rothschild went for £230, a dozen bottles of Château Lafite for £250 – rather like that scent at nine guineas an ounce that used to flavour pink Camay.

A man on crutches came in with a pretty girl holding a baby who started bellowing and was promptly removed. Like me, it was probably desperate for a drink.

Unable to stand any more talk about champagne, I moved over to a sale of Old Masters. The room was packed, the crowd really smelling of money: the women, suntanned, many of them chewing gum, wore those pale silk jersey dresses that cost such a fortune in dry-cleaning bills.

The auctioneer, a patrician Cyril Fletcher, had come-to-bid eyes and a spotted tie.

'Who's he?' I asked.

'The Chairman of Sotheby's,' whispered my neighbour. I felt slightly shocked – as though I'd gone into Marks and Spencer, and Mr Marks himself had risen from behind a counter and measured me for a bra. On the left were a chorus of aesthetes in coloured shirts and wide knotted ties, like a Harvie and Hudson window.

Bidding was brisk, a Crivelli madonna and a Jan de Heem still life going for vast sums. I can take or leave rare wines, but I really coveted some of those pictures. I felt a sudden longing to escape from the venal world of Bond Street into one of those shining, untroubled seventeenth-century landscapes and sleep on the grass or paddle knee-deep with the cows in one of those misty reed-strewn rivers.

Then an El Greco Christ came up for sale, and the atmosphere in the room changed electrically, eyes swivelling left to right, watching the chief bidders like a Wimbledon crowd.

Equally athletic were the eyebrows of the auctioneer recording bids, as they rose from £40,000 to £50,000. Was the huddled figure on the right going any higher? He shook his head. Everyone turned round, trying to read the thoughts of the dispassionate, ageless man on the left. His companion whispered to him, he nodded, the bidding rose to £51,000. There was a pause. The auctioneer looked round with polite incredulity. Was no one going any higher? Down came the gavel.

On to Sotheby's Belgravia to a sale of nineteenth–twentieth-century collector's items – all those lovely nostalgic toys like Bagatelle and Diabolo that one's grandmother used to unearth when one went to stay as a child.

The atmosphere here was much jollier than Bond Street, men in maroon overalls carting goods back and forth, surreptitiously playing with the toys as they waited. Suddenly a monkey bandsman would break into a frenzied tattoo, or a musical box open and a burst of tinkling notes come out.

A wooden ark went for £35, a clockwork mouse orchestra for £70.

I was dying to buy a clockwork goat with real fur which leapt from the ground. But I was too timid to start bidding, and it went unsold. A beautiful music box went for a considerable sum. Two assistants stepped forward to remove it, then both stepped back, thinking the other had hold of it. The box crashed to the floor, rosewood splintering, entrails and machinery spilling out. 'Sale cancelled,' sighed the auctioneer.

I was still kicking myself for not buying that goat when two men staggered on, carrying a vast early-twentieth-century carrier's sign of four horses pulling a wagon under a turquoise sky. 'Brighton and Maidstone' said the inscription on the picture.

It was too much of a coincidence. Maidstone is the name of our ludicrously doted-upon English setter, and I knew that regardless of size and price I had to have that painting.

Someone kicked off at £5. Rapidly the bidding rose to £12. Gingerly, I raised my hand. The auctioneer looked in my direction. Funking it, I hastily pretended to be brushing back my hair. An old biddy offered £15 and, determined not to be outbiddied, I caught the auctioneer's eye and nodded.

'Eighteen pounds – I'm bid.'

Then like a swimmer who plunges into an icy river and suddenly discovers he can crawl, I was off, bidding away like a maniac, winking, blinking and nodding. A terrible God-like feeling assailed me.

Unconcerned, I bid away the housekeeping money, then the paper bill. Away went the nanny's salary, and the money for my daughter's new shoes. The other bidders fell by the wayside. Only a girl in a peasant blouse with ebony curls was still in the race.

She raised the bid. I raised it. She raised it to a ludicrous sum.

None of us would eat for a week. Even the dog would have to survive on art alone, but the latent Guggenheim was unleashed in me. I made a higher bid, and waited, heart thumping.

It seemed an eternity. Then the black curls shook in defeat. Down came the gavel.

'Sold to the blonde,' said the auctioneer.

I was swinging from the chandeliers, felt as though I'd won the pools. That I was paying out a fortune rather than receiving one seemed quite irrelevant. 'Brighton and Maid-stone' was mine.

I looked across at the girl with black curls. Her shoulders slumped in disappointment and suddenly I felt terribly mean. Perhaps she had a dog at home called Brighton.

Birds of a Feather

Across the great continent of Africa still surges an irrepressible mass of tourists.

I love going abroad but I must confess I enjoy looking at other tourists just as much as the wildlife.

Even though a herd of elephants had come down to the waterhole in Tsavo, Kenya, I was far more interested in observing a middle-aged, middle-class English couple (Howard looks so nice in his paisley cravat) deliberately raising their voices over their gin and tonics so that the distinguished-looking other middle-aged, middle-class English couple sitting nearby would hear them and realise they were the right sort of people to get to know.

Our best tourist haul, however, was at a game lodge in the Meru Reserve. I was sitting quietly after dinner, eavesdropping on an American lady who'd been taping warthogs all afternoon. She was complaining to her friend that red ants had eaten all her Ex-Lax, and that she would like someone on the tour called Barbie much better if she didn't wear such 'jarring' shoes.

As she paused for breath, three zebra-striped buses drew up outside, and suddenly Reception was filled with hearty laughter, ringing voices, bald-headed, bespectacled men in long, loose shorts, and ladies with pink, unmade-up faces, open-necked shirts, and bare hairy legs going straight down into their canvas shoes.

There were twenty-five of them on an ornitholiday, bird-watching for fourteen days round Kenya.

'We're birdies, you know,' said an eager lady with plaits round her head, shaking hands with me. I half expected her to tickle my palm with a claw like a Freemason.

Later the occupants of the lodge watched fascinated as the birdies drew together four sofas in a square, and, sustained by swigs of orangeade, played a sort of bird bingo, all holding charts on which they listed the day's sightings. Their leader, who had a long nose and eyes set too close together but gleaming with conviction, did the calling. His voice was cockney pedantic like Peter Cook's in the *Dud and Pete* series.

'Anyone seen a grey-backed fiscal?' he said.

A lady with a rosy freckled face raised her hand: 'I did, coming out of *The Ark* this morning.'

'I saw a second one,' said a red-headed man with spectacles.

'You were present, if you recall, Geoffrey. They have grey on their backs, dirty grey.'

Everyone ticked dutifully.

'Very difficult to keep awake,' said a lady birdie wearing a hearing aid.

The leader looked disapproving.

'Page eighteen, column three,' he said, running his Biro with his name on down the list. 'No tits today, none at all.'

An elderly man with a walrus moustache cleared his throat:

'I am con-vinced,' he began.

'Any orioles?' said the leader, ignoring him.

'There was a black-winged-winged oriole,' said the lady with the ruddy freckled face.

'I am con-vinced,' began Walrus Moustache again.

'Wait your turn, Geoffrey,' said the leader bossily.

'Con-vinced I saw a pair of tits coming out of the gents' toilet, but they were too quick for me.'

'Any starling?' snapped the leader. 'I saw two blue-eared glossy from the vehicle. Are you happy with that, Keith?'

Everyone ticked, candlelight gleamed on the bald heads.

'Awfully difficult to keep awake,' boomed the lady with the hearing aid.

'All I've seen of interest is a red-knobbed coot,' said a pretty, sulky-looking girl who must have been thirty years younger than anyone else.

'Good for you, Cynthia,' said the leader, 'that was observant indeed.'

'I espied a yellow bishop,' said a woman with bare legs. 'He was flashing frantically in the back yard.'

'I, too, saw a yellow bishop coming out of the toilets,' said Geoffrey, his Adam's apple quivering, 'and a long-tailed widow coming down from *The Ark*.'

'I, too, saw a long-tailed widow,' said the leader, 'and weren't they nice, Geoffrey? The only thing a little disappointing was the tail, which is supposed to be nearly thirty inches in length, which it clearly was not.'

My husband and a game-warden friend, who'd drunk a fair amount of brandy by then, had to be forcibly restrained from saying 'cheep, cheep' all the time.

'I think I saw a white-bellied go-away-bird,' said an eager, mousy woman, blushing furiously.

'In deference to Susan,' said Geoffrey, his sunburnt knobbly knees blazing like traffic lights, 'I saw the same bird opposite me on top of a bush. I think it was a waxbill.'

'Hardly keep awake,' intoned the hearing-aid lady.

'Pair of tits by the gents,' said Walrus Moustache.

'Might have been a yellow-rumped seedeater, rather than a waxbill,' said the leader. 'Anyone seen anything else? All right, thank you very much. Breakfast at eight o'clock. How about a stroll before turning in, Geoffrey?'

After a restless night, we were woken at six by raucous cries from the birdies out on the lawn, field glasses raised.

'Good morning, Mary. Are you heading toward the breakfast room for some refreshment?'

'Yes indeed, Geoffrey. What is that dot in the sky?'

'A pygmy falcon, I suspect, Mary.'

Next moment Geoffrey had suddenly thrown himself down on his back on the dewy grass, holding his telescope up in heavily veined hands, propping it up on his raised leg to get a better view. A minute later three large ladies followed suit. My husband, coming out of his hut rather the worse for wear, nearly fell over them.

'I believe it's a kestrel,' said Geoffrey. 'Can you detect any tail feathers, Mary?'

I hid my face in the bougainvillea.

A lady birdie in beige slacks approached me.

'Are you a professional botanist?' she said. 'I gather that was a game warden you were dining with last night. It would be wonderful if I could introduce him to our leader.'

Breakfast was most unsettled. Every few minutes a birdie would utter a strangled squawk, then they would all throw down their spoons, and, cheeks bulging with All-Bran, charge through the French windows clutching their binoculars, crying, 'Anyone for terns?'

'Dear me,' I heard Keith saying, 'a fiscal has just excruciated on Daphne's sandal.'

'What Kitey did on whom from a great height,' muttered my husband.

Later in the day we passed them hanging out of the windows of their three zebra-striped buses, cajoling a very small rust and turquoise bird to Watch the Birdie. Fifteen yards away three stunningly beautiful giraffes floated by like a dream sequence, unheeded.

I suppose the essence of a good holiday is that it should be regurgitated in tranquillity – that to these intrepid travellers should present no problem. How many evenings in Kennington or Redhill will they not gladden with ciné of red-knobbed coot or yellow-rumped seedeater, or with tape recordings of feuding bishops or trilling fiscals?

Guest Appearances

I am not good at having people to stay. My name is not writ large among the heavenly hostesses.

'Of course you can have a bed,' I say in answer to that late-night telephone call. Usually a bed is all they get. With six people living in the house already, there are barely enough sheets for all of us. So I have to rush round at dead of night, whipping blankets off the children's beds, whereupon they wake up and protest vigorously. Eventually I take them off our bed instead, whereupon my husband, who is already lying morosely horizontal because a guest needed a second pillow, is totally unmollified by my suggestion that we have our love to keep us warm.

Having people to stay needs the kind of organisation we encountered last year in someone's house when we arrived for the weekend to find laid tables everywhere: in the kitchen for lunch, in the dining room for sixteen for dinner. Even my breakfast tray was laid ready for the morning. At 9.30 on the dot it arrived with a perfectly boiled brown egg with 'Friday' written on it, and a little pot of marmalade marked '75.

Of course it takes very special guests to put up with our house; it must be rather like staying in the zoo. I know from the first five minutes if the visit will be a disaster – if they give the dogs vertical pats which indicate 'go away, you smelly beast' rather than horizontal pats of approval. Or there are the guests who are allergic to cats, so the cat door gets blockaded with corrugated paper through which long, supplicating furry arms keep appearing.

Admittedly, things have improved since our flat days in Earl's Court, when guests had to share a box room with the piano, all the wedding presents we couldn't stand, my husband's cricket and rugger gear, and the lingering aroma of tomcat and the fifty-odd green milk bottles which had been hastily put outside the front door that morning.

Today our spare room doubles up with my husband's dressing room. So visiting aunts and nubile friends of my stepdaughter are sometimes startled at dawn by his rooting round for a matching pair of socks (or so he claims).

Another problem is that we only have a huge double bed in there, so the alternative for single-bed addicts is the bottom of my son's bunk bed. Recently we stayed with a couple whose marriage we heard was on the rocks. Our suspicions were confirmed when we found the husband's pyjamas at the bottom of our bed.

But one has to take so many precautions before having people to stay – luring the children outside so Uncle Willy's excruciating watercolour of springer spaniels in bracken can be removed from behind the nursery door and exchanged for the Herring over the fireplace in the drawing room. Meanwhile praying my husband won't ask me in front of Uncle Willy whether I'm having the Herring cleaned.

Or carefully extracting the hard porn from the spareroom shelves before Aunt Maud arrives. It's intriguing the way the same books crop up in spare rooms: the latest Elizabeth Jane Howard, the yachtsman's weekend book, a guide to roses, and Alex Comfort's latest sex primer *pour encourager les oats*.

Then the guests arrive in a flurry of chocolates, and flowers which I jam in a vase, vowing to arrange later, but never do. The first night of the visit usually goes well. Everyone drinks too much and staggers to bed.

'I want you to lie in,' I say firmly, which, roughly translated, means for God's sake don't get up until I've got my head together, straightened the kitchen, and cleaned the dogs' hairs off the sofa.

Alas no one can lie in when the children are up at seven executing some manic Carthorse Lake on the top floor over the spare room. Consequently guests are down fully dressed by 8.30, asking if the 22 bus goes to Kew Gardens. As I am incapable of carrying on such Aldous Huxley house-party conversations while getting breakfast the result is burnt toast and frizzled bacon.

'But I like my eggs well done,' said my mother-in-law, gallantly trying to force buckling toast soldiers into bullet-hard eggs. Invariably, too, I forget to turn on the washing-up machine the night before, so we have nothing to eat with or off.

But breakfast over – what the hell do you do with guests for the rest of the day? One advantage of a large house party must be that guests, like children, amuse each other – a pity one can't put them in a playpen until one is ready. As a result meals get earlier and earlier, beginning with a glass of sherry at eleven, followed by lunch at twelve, tea at 3.30, whereupon I ponder on the possibility of a cold collation at 5.45 to fill in the time until my husband gets back from work.

Having people to stay is always easier at weekends when he can entertain, while I bustle. I'm lucky too – he's domesticated. Other husbands are merely handy about the house guest, pouncing on you every time the hostess's back is turned, waking you at dawn with early-morning teeth.

But the worst thing from any guest's point of view is when the hostess's affability starts wearing thin, and you've still got time to go before your scheduled departure. How often on country weekends around Sunday drinks time have I seen that muscle flickering in my hostess's cheek, like the warning light on a car running out of petrol?

Usually at this point she grimly thrusts the visitors' book into my hand, hoping I'll redeem myself by writing something witty and pointing out, 'George Melly was here last week, and did the most hilarious drawing.'

But my mind goes blank as I gaze and gaze on those rows of signatures from SW1, SW2, SW3.

Gideon and Samantha Molesworth-Bellow, Thurloe Square.

Miss Fiona Molesworth-Bellow, ditto, adding in round schoolgirl hand: 'Simply super propheteroles'.

Fortunately affability is usually restored on the point of departure, when the whole family line up to bid farewell, the host stooping to remove groundsel from the front garden, the children waving the dog's paw, the hostess totally forgetting that a few minutes ago she never wanted to see her guests again, crying:

'It's been far too short, come again for a really proper visit next time, and bring the children, our smalls would love to entertain them, no, the best way's up the M4, goodbye, goodbye . . . don't stop waving till they get out of sight, darling . . . oh hell, they've left their gumboots behind.'

The Biggest Classroom in the World

I have always loved wild flowers. One of the joys of my childhood was setting out on summer afternoons with my mother, certain for an hour or two of her undivided attention, and wandering down by the river, blowing dandelion clocks, searching for four-leaved clovers, and trying to gauge the weather from the scarlet pimpernel. Above my head, huge as trees, towered the majestic hogweed, as I ran along tunnels forged through the long grass by the blackberry pickers.

Only recently, however, since I've been walking dogs on Putney Common, have wild flowers become a passion. In an unreliable world, there is something comfortingly reliable that each spring the kittenish purple and yellow faces of the heartsease appear round the same gravestone in Barnes graveyard, and that each August the toadflax will bloom on the same place by the football pitch. Half my books are now marked by pressed flowers. In my copy of Keats, a sorrel leaf keeps its brilliant crimson after three seasons, while the willow herb in my diary has faded to an amethyst remembrance of the gaudy rose-mauve it was when picked.

Every ramble, too, becomes a treasure hunt. There was a walk in June when the wild garlic made Fountains Abbey smell like a Soho restaurant. I shall always remember a *Reader's Digest* walk through Hambledon woods as the first time I found wild marjoram and Aaron's rod.

I'm still pretty ignorant as a botanist. I am always ferreting around in some textbook for the identity of a plant, but by next week, I've forgotten it. I've looked up redlegs and fat hen about ten times this summer. More often I pick flowers, but forget to look them up when I get home, and by the time I remember they're limp unrecognisable potpourri at the bottom of my bag.

Even so, I love reading flower books. The list of contents sounds like the *dramatis personae* at the beginning of a nineteenth-century novel. There are the Goosefoot family, the Saxifrage family, the St John's Worts; imagine the glamour of an upper-class rake called Jakey St John's Wort.

Or there are the Broomrape family, who are 'parasites and can be distinguished from their relations the Toothworts by

their long narrow teeth', which sounds like the beginning of
a horror movie.

Guidebooks are excellent, too, at cutting the most lovely-
sounding flowers down to size. The rose of Sharon, for
example, is listed as 'a creeping medium evergreen under-
shrub'.

Take the book to the plant, say the naturalists, but that
doesn't help. My Collins guide only deals in centimetres so I
can never tell what height a plant should be, and I've been
mad with frustration all summer trying to identify a beastly
purplish-looking nettle, which seems to be either black hore-
hound, or the hedge woundwort, which are both described
in my book as 'tall hairy perennials up to 3 feet with an
unpleasant smell'.

And there are other problems. While I was trying to distinguish the nipplewort from all the other poor relations of
the dandelion family the other day, the dogs sneaked off and
into Putney Hospital. The result was a real 'Carry On' chase
round the wards, with me clutching my nipplewort and my
shrieking daughter pursuing the dogs and being in turn pur-
sued by a horde of enraged medics in white coats.

The drawings in guidebooks are marvellous, too, with
their delicate shapes and rainbow colours. Even in the

middle of winter, I can pore for hours over Keble Martin or the *Oxford Book of Wild Flowers*, dreaming that one day I may have the luck to find a fritillary or even a butterfly iris. Then impatiently, like a footballer waiting for September and the season to start, I begin looking out in February for first arrivals, the coltsfoot or the wild daffodils. Then in a rush comes the blackthorn, blossoming bravely and too early, its sooty branches looking as though they have been dipped in flour overnight, within days the candles on the chestnuts are lit up, followed shortly by the hawthorns exploding like great creamy rockets, then lacy mounds of cow parsley, and finally the elder, like one white wedding, crowding in upon another.

Now, in September, the common has reached an unkempt whiskery stage, rather like an ageing lady who's suddenly given in and decided not to bother about superfluous hair any more. Everywhere thistles are oozing kapok, willow herb a mass of down, sorrel rusting, nettles yellowing.

But there's still plenty of interest. As Geoffrey Grigson pointed out in his marvellous book *The Englishman's Flora*: 'Plants provided nine-tenths of the materials for medicine in the olden days.' On the common today, I found yarrow, which once healed wounds, burdock, which was supposed to have cured Henry III of syphilis, mugwort, which if dried and infused in water was considered an excellent tranquilliser during the menopause. Under an ivy-covered wall I found some comfrey, which medieval doctors swore relieved backache caused by too much sex. And in the graveyard were swathes of periwinkle which if worn round the thigh were regarded as a deterrent against miscarriage.

Practically every plant in existence seems to have been used as a laxative. If inflation gets any worse, we shall soon be practising our own floral medicines. The Health Service administrators had better look to their laurels. Even laurel, it seems, was once believed to cure flatulence and influenza.

Half the charm of wild flowers of course is their smell. I think I could find my way round the common blindfold, guided by the sweet vanilla scent of the bindweed by the bowling green, or the 'heavenly breath' of the wild roses or the soapy smell of the hawthorns. Even a plant as ugly and treacherous as the stinging nettle gives off the most seductively heady smell after a shower of rain.

I've always been fascinated, too, by the legends surrounding flowers. The dandelion, for example, is believed to have sprung from the dust raised by the chariot of the sun, which is why it opens at dawn and closes at dusk.

Then there are the superstitions. Hawthorn is beloved in France, where wedding guests carry sprigs into church to bring happiness to the bride and groom. But in England, most people think it unlucky and refuse to have it in the house. You also get the ambiguous nature of a plant like traveller's joy, which lifts the heart in autumn with its shining festoons, yet can turn a copse into a jungle and choke a young tree to death. It has such a beautiful name, like so many wild flowers: wolfsbane, deadly nightshade, Venus's looking-glass, foxglove; one can imagine a fox drawing on sleek purple gloves like a burglar before raiding a hencoop. And finally there's restharrow, a little yellow vetch with roots so tough they wound round the ancient ploughs and brought the oxen to a standstill.

And so I go on learning a little of what country people have known for generations. When I take my children on the Common and show them the fairy shoes in the lip of the white nettle, and hold buttercups under their chins to see if they like butter, and play soldiers with the plantain, I feel a great happiness in imparting to them the magic of generations in a classroom, which as Kenneth Allsop once said, 'has no walls'.

Perils of a Parrot Sitter

August is a wicked month – particularly for pets. All over the country dogs droop at the closing of holiday suitcases, last-minute instructions for feeding the guinea pigs are hastily scrawled for the daily woman and, as families pile merrily into estate cars bound for Estoril and Marbella, anxious furry faces appear at the window wondering if they've been abandoned for ever.

But wretched as it is for the pets left behind, it's almost more traumatic for the animal sitters left in charge of them. How do you face people returning euphoric from holiday with the news that the gerbil has snuffed it and the goldfish are floating on their sides at the top of the tank?

One friend was asked to parrot-sit over a weekend. On Sunday she ran out of bird seed and, improvising brilliantly, gave the parrot a high tea of Alpen, whereupon it keeled over and had to be rushed to the RSPCA intensive care unit and drip-fed for a fortnight.

Worse still, another chum was left in charge of someone's house in Kenya, during which time the dog was eaten by a lion, the horse jumped out of its field and broke a leg, the swimming pool developed algae, the tennis court went bald, and the unmarried cook and the rabbit gave unexpected birth simultaneously.

I never have such gruelling experiences myself. Usually it's just ten minutes' fiddling to locate the right key, and the neighbours' cats weaving reproachfully down the banister, mewing piteously over the uneaten plates of Kit-e-Kat and yesterday's milk with its yellowing rim and a few black hairs floating on top.

Last week, however, I graduated to looking after a neighbour's ducks and hens, with dire consequences. Arriving on Saturday morning, nervously mixing the duck food – 'not too sloppy but not too stiff or they'll seize' – I went into the garden to find the ducks had been seized already. Not a trace anywhere, except for feathers and a few fox prints located by my son on the lawn. For the next two hours, like Duckless Fairbanks, we swashbuckled our way through the dense rain-soaked undergrowth of neighbouring gardens, forlornly crying Dilly Dilly. But no such duck.

We couldn't find the house cat either, until faint distracted mewing told us he was locked in the owners' bedroom. Having failed to break the door down, my husband suggested feeding very thin slices of smoked salmon under the door. Finally we found a locksmith called Death, which the poor cat must have been feeling like by the time he was liberated. The bedroom wasn't in any too hygienic a state either.

At least the hens were alive and clucking. But next day, crawling in search of the ducks again, I emerged from the herbaceous border so precipitously that the hens took fright and fluttered straight through their plastic netting. Trying to get hens back into a run is not unlike those infuriating glass-topped games in which you have to edge six ball bearings into golf holes. Both my temper and the plastic netting were in shreds by the time they were safely rehoused.

In dread I waited for the owner to return.

'I don't know how to begin,' I stammered. 'There's your bedroom and the locksmith's bill, and the hens have gone broody and the poor little ducks . . .'

'Oh, I forgot to tell you,' she said, 'we took the ducks with us.'

Looking after people's dogs is a problem, as they can't be left *in situ* like cats. A friend is currently housing a tight-skinned curly-tailed mongrel called Rover, who's a compulsively slow walker. She feels such an idiot bellowing to him on the Common when all the other dog walkers are yelling out chic dog names like Brunhilda and Melchester.

Then there are the impeccably behaved but gently melancholic Labradors boarded out in country houses while their masters serve in Northern Ireland and Germany. One black Labrador I know is such a good gun dog, she keeps being asked to stay in Scotland without her master. One feels she ought to arrange for a human sitter to bring him bottles of whisky while she's away.

I don't mind looking after people's pets short term. What I do find insidious is the way our house is being turned into an animal refugee camp. Once upon a peaceful time, we had only two cats, one tabby and one black, and intended to keep it that way. Then a girlfriend invited me to lunch 'for a lovely gossip' at Bianchi's. She was waiting at the table with a fluffy black tomcat on a lead.

'Oh, how sweet,' I said – fatally.

'I know,' she said, her huge eyes filling with tears, 'and I'm moving in with Ron tonight, and his landlady won't allow pets.'

By the end of a carafe of wine, and several silly jokes about her inability to tell right from Ron, I found myself the owner of the black cat. Back home to ferocious resistance from incumbent cats, growling retreats under dressers, and the furniture covered with buttered paw marks.

Then in April this year, a friend who owns yet another black cat announced she was getting married and moving into a small flat in Kensington.

'Just think how the little cat will miss a garden,' she said wistfully.

I won't listen, I thought frantically, but once again heard myself agreeing that earth boxes and newly-wedded bliss didn't really go together. By the end of the evening, another victim of a put-together home had joined our menagerie.

This particular cat, scared to face the paw-swiping that accompanies meals downstairs, insists on being fed in our bedroom – spit level, my husband calls it. He is less amused when, rising groggily at dawn, he plunges his heel into a saucer of Whiskas.

Not that he has a cat-encrusted foot to stand on. Last week he telephoned from the office.

'The pub cat was going to be put down.'

'Where is he now?' I said sternly.

'Asleep in my pending tray.'

So now we have four black cats, and my days are spent trying to distinguish one from the other. I know how mothers of identical quads suffer. The pub cat, a strapping tom with a right hook which even the dog respects, has settled in a treat. He sleeps in a box of fireworks on top of the oven, and descends like an atom tom whenever I plunge the tin-opener even into a can of tomatoes. Each time I unearth the chopping board even for onions, I am overwhelmed by a tidal wave of black bodies squirming sycophantically in anticipation of liver.

The financial aspect is crippling, too, as every day crates of cat food arrive.

I know I shouldn't grumble. According to a ludicrous *Which?* survey, the average cat gives its owner 1 hour 40 minutes' pleasure a day, which, with five cats, means 8 hours 20 minutes. Add to that another 3½ hours, which is alleged to be the amount of pleasure provided by our medium-sized dog (he's incensed, evidently small dogs and large dogs rate 4 hours each), and the total per day is 11 hours 50 minutes of pleasure. It's too much. As Shaw pointed out, 'A lifetime of happiness! No man alive could bear it.'

I suppose I should be glad, as the textbooks tell me, to have a unique opportunity to study the domestic cat in a colony situation. But where will it end? Like an alcoholic trying to avoid the pub, I scuttle past the pet shop. But my eyes are irresistibly drawn to the door where beneath a sign saying, 'Please remove your crash helmet before entering, it frightens the parrot', is a small, sad little notice:

'Due to bereavement,' says the loopy writing, 'a home is needed for Fluff, a black and white doctored tom. Fluff is lovable and clean.'

Avert the eyes, walk on, faster, faster, faster.

Double-decker Mummies

Of my grandparents, I remember my mother's mother best. A beauty even to the end, she had rose-petal skin, innocent blue eyes and swept-up white hair, with a rakish blonde streak at the front from chain-smoking. She perfectly fitted Wordsworth's description of an old lady: 'Serene and bright, and lovely as a Lapland night.'

Most of her time was spent reading novels: Jane Austen, Thackeray, Mrs Henry Wood, holding the book on top of a pair of combinations. If anyone came into the room, she would hastily whip the combinations over the book and pretend to be sewing.

Good works were not really her forte but, being a clergyman's wife, she made a great effort. On one occasion, my aunt surreptitiously added the dog's and cat's names to her prayer list, and the entire Mothers' Union were exhorted in a ringing voice to pray for Raggety Bones and Mewkins.

Intensely gentle, a great giggler and a chronic pessimist (she would never admit to being anything better than 'fairly well, darling'), she was teased and yet adored by all her grandchildren. She in turn sent us fruit cake and wrote us long illegible letters at school. My cousin, aged eight, remembers curling up in embarrassment when his form master deciphered one of them in front of the whole class: 'I saw Mummy today,' he read, then turning over two pages by mistake, 'she has a long black fluffy tail, and green eyes.'

Like the best grannies, she was a great character, as was one of my husband's grandmothers, who read *The Times* every day in asbestos gloves and, at the age of eighty-three, smashed the drawing-room chandelier with her walking stick demonstrating how Arnold Palmer should have played an iron shot. Her funeral, too, was fitting. During the cremation service, the record got stuck on 'Abide Abide Abide with Me', which would have made her cackle with laughter. Afterwards everyone repaired to her house and had a rip-roaring party on Australian burgundy unearthed from the cellar.

Attitudes towards grandmothers vary from country to country of course. In France, the grand-mère lives in the same house, ruling despotically over a vast family. The English tend to put her in a home, or a Tunbridge Wells boarding house, and forget her except for the occasional pilgrimage of avarice if she happens to be rich.

The young have been adulated in this country for so long that I suspect the pendulum is swinging back and the grandmother is about to become a cult figure. We live in such confused times that suddenly grandparents as a symbol of marital stability and old-world standards have become very attractive.

The Queen, for example, after a triumphant Jubilee year, is about to become a grandmother, so probably over the next few years will Mrs Thatcher, Shirley Williams, Antonia Fraser, even Brigitte Bardot.

For most of us the ideal grandmother is a cosy, twinkling-eyed Mrs Tiggy Winkle figure and, fortunately for most women, the thrill of having grandchildren seems amply to compensate for a superficially ageing image. Can one be a grandmother and a *grande horizontale* at the same time, though? Certainly one can in fiction – there's a new book just out called *The Love Habit* entirely devoted to the gallivantings of an erotomaniac granny.

The biggest excitement seems to be when one's daughter has her first baby: 'I never dreamt how overjoyed I'd feel,' said one young granny. 'As though I was having a baby of my own without the birth pains. I could never understand why people spoiled their grandchildren so much, but once it happens you hold this little thing in your arms and suddenly you're aware of immortality, of life growing on through you on a bigger scale. You have this incredible sense of the flow of time, of having one's own stake in eternity.'

Or, as my daughter said in a moment of lucidity, a granny is just a double-decker mummy.

All blessings, however, are mixed blessings and having achieved the miracle of a grandchild, the grandmother's next problem is to keep her trap shut. 'You feel the baby is not being looked after exactly as you would wish,' said one. 'In my day we washed nappies and didn't automatically pick up a child when it started crying. But you bite your tongue off not to interfere.'

The wolf dressed up as a grandmother perhaps wasn't such a fairy tale.

'What big eyes you've got, Granny!'

'All the better to see where Mummy's going wrong in bringing you up, darling.'

Visits to grandparents, particularly when children are in the roughhousing stage, can be murder – all those footballs snapping the regalia lilies, and sticky little hands stretching out for the Rockingham. Mealtimes are often a nightmare too.

'Why do all my grandchildren eat as though they're gardening?' said one granny. To which her grandchild, who was examining the wrinkles, replied: 'And why have you got a striped face, Granny?'

A grandmother, of course, is also a mother-in-law, and unless she has a relaxed and affectionate relationship with her daughter-in-law, the grandchildren, inheriting their mother's animosity, will tend to prefer the maternal grandmother to the paternal one. I adored my paternal grandmother, but I was always in awe of her. I suspect it was because the tension and desire to prove herself as a good wife and mother that my mother displayed in my grandmother's presence was transmitted to me even as a small baby.

Invariably there's rivalry between grandmothers, a sort of granny-mosity; not just larger hats at the christening but a very natural desire to be loved best. My children always get a kick on the ankles when they muddle Granny Brighton and Granny 'Orkshire on the telephone.

'I was staying with my daughter for the weekend,' admitted one granny, 'and the children made a terrific fuss of me, then suddenly my son-in-law's mother arrived and they were all over her. It's so undignified to sulk at my age.'

A grandmother also tends to prefer the eldest grandchild on both sides. She has known them longer and therefore better. Often when a second child is born and the limelight shifts from the first child, it turns to its grandparents for the extra spoiling and understanding it needs.

In fact grandparents and grandchildren seem to get on better left on their own. Two generations are company, three's a crowd. Just as Granny's aware of the flow of time when her grandchild is born, grandchildren in turn are fascinated by their roots; it gives them a sense of belonging to hear anecdotes of the old days, of Uncle Willy's peccadilloes and how naughty Mummy and Daddy were when they were children.

Together they can revel in first and second childhoods and they do have the same enchanting tendency towards malapropisms. My son came back from a trip to Battle Abbey in July saying he'd had a lovely time 'exploring a middle-aged castle'. Five minutes later my mother rang up. 'Wasn't it wonderful, darling, Virginia Woolf winning Wimbledon.'

Swallows and Amazons

It was hen night at The Horseshoes Pub in Wandsworth on Wednesday. And I now know all about sisterhood. Apart from the joy of spending an evening with 200 women, there was the added incentive of two male strippers, called Sailor and Jack the Lad, assorted drag artists, chicken and chips and a free drink for only £4. 'Hen nights is very, very popular,' warned the landlord beforehand, 'so get there early.'

Certainly when I rolled up twenty minutes before opening time, the queue outside the Horseshoes went halfway down the street. Nervously I attached myself to a chattering group of married women.

'What did Kev say when you said you was going to a strip?' asked one blonde.

'He said, tch,' said her friend.

At seven o'clock, flashing lights were turned on, and in we trooped, jostling, cackling, exuberant with anticipation. The front runners bagged the best tables round the richly red-carpeted stage. On the scarlet-flocked walls, double bridles and snaffles gleaming in the rosy light looked suspiciously like instruments of sexual torture.

Muscular henchmen with broad shoulders, incredibly slim waists and jutting bums whizzed about fixing recording equipment, and nearly gouging out one's eyes with coat-hanger hooks, as they carried in glittering armfuls of sequinned dresses. One Greek God had so many swallows tattooed on his arms, it was a migration every time he passed.

The women were now queuing up for their free drink. Apart from a hard core of old cockney stalwarts who never took off their coats, the standard of female talent was staggeringly high.

'Men never bother on stag nights,' said the manager. 'But the ladies always dress up to the nines for a hen night.'

Most glamorous of all and at least seven feet tall from her rhubarb-pink, backcombed hair to her seven-inch heels was a drag queen called Rusty, who lounged against the bar in black lace slashed to the groin, and rapaciously eyed the Greek God covered in swallows.

All the front seats were taken, so I edged into a lone chair beside a party of secretaries, who gazed into space and were obviously determined to make their free drink last all night. One pretty girl, who ate so many crisps you felt she'd crunch at the touch, said she felt very nervous about the strippers. She wished she hadn't come, because her boyfriend felt so 'threatened'.

To my right was a much jollier bunch of Wandsworth regulars in leather coats called Doreen, Mary, Mary, Treena, Margaret and Jean. 'Your first hen night,' they said incredulously. 'You *will* enjoy it.'

Without the inhibiting presence of men, a fantastic camaraderie was building up.

There was a burst of music, and Rusty teetered on to the stage. 'Any girls not been to an 'en night before?' he drawled in his sepulchral baritone. A handful of women cautiously raised their hands. 'Well, 'ands up the virgins then.'

Two tables in front, a goaty-looking blonde shot up both her hands, to cackles of mirth from her friends.

The microphone gave an ear-splitting screech.

'That's nice,' smirked Rusty, as the Greek God bounded on to the stage to adjust it, 'this young man's coming to play with my nobs.' (More shrieks of mirth.)

After a few sexist jokes, Rusty introduced his 'very good friend, Norman Cable', another drag queen with ginger curls.

'Nice to see smiling faces,' said Norman, his lascivious Molly Parkin eyes roving over the audience. 'Left all the bastards at 'ome, 'ave you?'

A great cheer went up. He then launched into a string of anti-male jokes, so filthy but funny that even the nearby secretaries stopped munching crisps and let out the occasional nervous giggle.

After a particularly blue crack, there was a commotion, and three cockney stalwarts waddled to the door, chuntering furiously, demanding to be let out.

'What's up with them?' I asked.

'Got the wrong day,' explained Doreen, Mary and Mary. 'They thought it was an Irish night.'

Rusty now shimmered on in peacock-blue sequins, and announced the imminent approach of Sailor, the first stripper. The excitement was not so much sexual as the feverish anticipation of children on Christmas Eve.

The group of probation officers and social workers in the front row looked very apprehensive. There was a roll of drums. One of the social workers turned green. 'I know he's going to wave it in my face,' she squeaked, and bolted out to the loo.

Clutching my bag like a chastity belt, I took her seat. Fortunately, frenzied smoking had reduced the visibility to about three feet.

'I want you all to put your hands together for fabulous Sailor,' screamed Rusty, going completely over the top like Kermit.

Next moment, a plump young man with rosy cheeks, wearing a white sailor suit and a little sailor hat, erupted into the room in a frenzy of jolliness, rather like Percy Grainger in the Delius film. Pulling one of the social workers to her feet, he rotated his pelvis against her, then gathered up a grey-haired woman in a spotted dress, and carried her screaming delightedly round the room. Casting her aside, he seized the reluctant hand of another social worker and pressed her until she'd removed his little hat.

He then bounded across the tables, sending typists diving under their chairs, and now, horrors, he was advancing like the pantomime cat down the front row again. Rushing up to a pretty probation officer on my right, he thrust her hand down his trousers. She gave a gasp, then giggled, and drew out a red lollipop. With shaking hands, I just managed to undo one button and was presented with an orange lollipop.

Lil from Balham, however, who was on my left, was livid, when after undoing three buttons, she was only rewarded with a green one.

'I hate lime flavour,' she said indignantly.

A blue-rinsed pensioner was now briskly removing his trousers, like a nanny stripping a tired child. Gym shoes came off next, followed by his shirt, to reveal a charging elephant tattooed all over his chest, and he was down to the Union Jack pants.

'Get them off,' yelled the crowd.

He did, but underneath was another pair of Union Jack pants, and then another, and then another, driving the crowd to a frenzy.

Suddenly he turned his back, and whisked his pants down to half-mast to reveal one heavily lashed eye tattooed on each cheek. The room collapsed in hysterical laughter. The lights dimmed, the drums rolled. For a second, he stood totally naked then he scampered off to wild applause.

'I prefer the Scarlet Pimpernel,' said Lil. ''E does flame-throwing as well.'

In the queue for the loo, monumental boasting was going on. 'His winkle weren't nearly as big as my Norman's,' said a hoary old cockney loudly. 'Nor as big as my Stan's neither,' said her friend. 'I shall tell Stan, then he won't feel so threatened.'

'And Anna Raeburn claims size is immaterial,' sighed a social worker.

After such excitement, we fell on our chicken and chips. It was my luck to be accosted by a dissenting voice, a bossy-boots in a trouser suit.

'Don't you realise what a big thing it is for women,' she said earnestly, 'to have a night out away from their husbands? Don't you get a wonderful feeling of sisterhood?'

Seeing four large Bloody Marys lined up for me by Doreen, Mary and Mary, I said I did, and sidled off to talk to Sailor, who was now propping up the bar. He was a nice young man with the sort of sweet smile adored by mothers-in-law. We'd been a lovely, warm audience, he said, but then hen nights were always more appreciative than cock and hen nights.

'You can go as far as you like with just ladies,' he added. 'It's only when their old men come, too, they get scared to laugh, and you have to tone down your act.'

How did he do that? Oh, he let the men pick out the lollipops.

Drag artist followed drag artist, the music grew louder, noses shone, Carmen curls drooped. Visibility was down to two feet now. On every table was a forest of glasses. The bar takings must have been stupendous. The evening was due to end at eleven, and it was now five to, with still no sign of the second stripper, Jack the Lad. The audience were getting restless, worrying what their husbands would say.

I took refuge against the bar with Balham Lil. But instead of Jack the Lad, we got yet another drag artist, Danny O'Dell, who was, mercifully, extremely funny. 'I love those beautiful clothes,' sighed Lil, as off came his silver lurex shirt, leaving massive red, yellow and green plus-fourteens underneath. He then very slowly unearthed from them a cat's tail, a gherkin, a feather duster, a tickling stick, a fox fur, a rubber cockerel, a vast cucumber, and copious other sexual aids.

'So predictable,' said the dissenting bossy-boots scornfully.

He was drawing out a nine-foot pink rubber snake, when my minicab driver arrived to collect me. One glance at the stage and the audience, and the happy smile froze on his face. He fled like Actaeon into the night.

Finally the drums rolled even more thunderously, and on came Jack the Lad, who turned out to be the Greek God, covered in swallows, who'd been humping equipment, now wearing a black silk shirt, green trousers and high black boots.

'Good old Barbara,' screamed a group of secretaries, as he selected an eager middle-aged woman from their ranks and kissed her with such dumper-like force I thought he'd pull her teeth out. After a scamper round the tables, he made the mistake of asking the bossy-boots to undo one of his shirt buttons. With one bound, she was on him, whipping off his shirt (you half expected a flock of swallows to fly out) and scrabbling frantically at his trousers and pants.

'I only asked for one button,' he hissed, recoiling in horror. 'Don't mess me up, you'll ruin my act.'

Radiant with self-importance, she returned to her party. 'The big phoney! You could tell how threatened he felt.'

'Strippers is very shy people,' said Balham Lil reprovingly.

Jack was now down to a black satin jockstrap, rather like a Jane Austen reticule. One had to confess, he was wonderfully constructed. As the lights dimmed, he lit three flaming torches and ran them over his bronzed sweating chest and thighs, before bravely swallowing them. A smell of singeing hung on the air. The audience, now whipped up to a frenzy, were standing on tables and stamping their feet.

'Off, off, off,' they screamed.

Obediently Jack the Lad draped himself in a blue towel, and whipped off his final defence. Then, as a codpiece de résistance, he rotated his member round and round at a great speed like an English setter's tail. Then, even more brilliant, he turned his back on us, and went on rotating through his legs. A quick frontal whirl, back went the towel, and it was all over. I embraced Doreen, Mary and Mary and Co., and vowed to meet at the next hen night. Outside, a row of husbands stood patiently waiting on the pavement. Even my minicab driver had returned.

'Expect they're hoping for some side effects,' said Lil, going cackling into the night. It had been a marvellous evening. Happily I motored home to Putney, planning to write a stirring tale about Sister Hood and her band of merry hens.

Au bored de la mère

I'm not wild about holidays – they always seem a ludicrously expensive way of proving there's no place like home. The children, however, were getting upstaged in the playground by all their little friends with Seychellois suntans and, as a working wife, I had a craving to have the family to myself for a week, so I persuaded my husband to pile everyone into the car for an out-of-season week in France, *au bord de la mer*.

Friday: Usual eve-of-holiday panic, as I pack in a cupboard so as not to upset the dog. Choice of wardrobe limited by total failure of pre-holiday crash diets, and writer's brown, which consists of mahogany top half from typing in the garden and pale mauve legs. Even so, my clothes rise like a soufflé above the top of our suitcase. Is my husband's jaundiced air due to the fact that he hasn't put any clothes in yet, or because I've been wearing the same old sweater and skirt all week?

'You do realise,' he says grimly, 'it won't be a rest.'

'It'll be a break,' I say cheerfully, throwing fifteen novels into a carrier bag. 'All that lovely food and early nights because we won't have a babysitter, and anyway children always adore the seaside.'

Saturday: Children up at dawn wild with excitement. Usual row because my husband, knowing I won't be ready at agreed time of ten o'clock, starts revving up the car at nine fifty-five. Muscles still going like indicators in both our jaws when we reach Dover. Good humour restored by first euphoric brandy on the ferry. My husband converts our money into francs on a sick bag, which he will no doubt need when he sees how low the rate of exchange is.

Motor to Arras, watering at the mouth at prospect of first French dinner. Alas hors d'œuvre comes out of a tin, and coq au vin tastes principally of Oxo. Heavy wine-drugged sleep wrecked by my daughter's complaints that the dark is not light enough.

Sunday: Interminable drive, stopping at inevitable war graveyards through the Somme. The poplars wave muffs of mistletoe, the sun shines through the mist like a dog's identity disc. Reverie about the beauty of countryside rudely interrupted by my husband asking for directions through

Rouen. No red-kneed poisonous Mexican spider could instil more terror than does the map of Rouen spreading out like some vile tarantula flexing its legs in *toutes directions*. An extremely tense hour later, after I have misrouted us on to the Paris, Beauvais, Dieppe and even Calais roads, we land quite by chance on the right road.

Arrive at Arromanches, centre of the D-Day landings; the caissons used in the Mulberry Harbour still rise from the sea like blackened teeth. Despite icy gales, and grey agitated waves, the children are avid to bathe. The beach is strewn with dead jellyfish and large French ladies with Mia Farrow hairstyles — tremble at the thought of how many more of both must be lurking in the sea. Assure my daughter, through chattering teeth, it is quite safe.

Next moment a huge wave drenches us. My daughter exits, sobbing noisily. My son unearths a rusty bicycle wheel from a rock pool and asks me if it is worf anything. My husband, appalled by the lack of talent, goes off to the D-Day Museum. Huddle, hiding red and purple legs under a towel, observing how unfair it is that magenta legs look perfectly all right on a seagull. In an incredibly short time, all our clothes, towels, books, combs and bathing things are thickly encrusted with wet sand, which I say brightly will come off when everything dries. Alas, nothing ever does. There is no heating in the hotel rooms. Also it seems the ultimate in male chauvinism that hotels always have points for razors but never for hairdriers. After a brief dip, my tangled mane resembles an hysterical bird's nest. Now I understand all the Mia Farrow hairstyles. Later, unexpectedly bump into the editor of the *Sunday Times* – is there no escape for either of us!

Monday: Even children agree it is too cold to bathe. Learn that there is a limited time even children can spend building sandcastles and popping seaweed. During gloomy picnic, my husband complains he has lumbago, a cold and gut-ache. 'Crock Monsieur,' I say. My joke falls as heavily as a pétanque ball.

Moules for dinner. The children and I have about six helpings each, which my husband says darkly we will regret later. Our bedroom is now deep in sand like the Sahara. Fed up with sartorial restrictions imposed by purple legs, I put on overnight tanning cream. Woken yet again from drugged sleep by sound of my son being sick in a face towel. Sandcastle bucket comes in most useful for subsequent attacks which go on till dawn. Now realise why my husband goes on about

Normandy landings, having spent all night racing along one trying to reach lavatory with sick bucket before light goes out.

Tuesday: Appalled to see overnight tanning cream has turned the sheets the colour of tomato soup. Slink out of hotel, praying maid will not think it my bizarre digestion. Long drive into Brittany to Sable d'Or les Pins, a 'resort' where I happily stayed with my parents twenty-five years ago. Get more and more nervous, as we approach, that it will have gone off. Arrive as shadows are lengthening. Fear that we may not find a hotel makes us book into first one sighted, which turns out to be a Virginia-creepered borstal crawling with English and surrounded by Rover 2000s.

Drink in lounge before dinner surrounded by gloomy whispering fellow countrymen. Why do the English abroad always behave as though they're at a funeral? Probably because all the husbands like mine are hissing to their wives not to smile at anyone in case they get 'involved'. Tell children not to eat too many crisps so as not to ruin their dinner. Alas, dinner already ruined by chef, who has bland tastelessness of food in expensive nursing homes: *Potage Bonne Femme*, followed by boiled fish, followed by some kind of boiled chicken.

Roused yet again by my daughter, frightened of the dark. Turn on side light, whereupon my son wakes and complains he can't sleep with light on, which in turn wakes couple in next room, who bang loudly on wall, which wakes my husband, who says turn the bloody light off, and he supposes that's another night's sleep gone. Next hour spent listening to counterpoint of my daughter's muffled sobs and my husband's gentle snoring. Rest of night spent wondering how large families living in one room ever became large families.

Wednesday: What I imagined to be romantic rustling of poplars outside our window turns out to be steady downpour which doesn't let up for the rest of our stay. So fat from misery eating, whatever way I put on my pants they feel back to front. Read copy of *Elle* found in wastepaper basket which says *une vraie beauté sauvage* is fashionable this autumn. Glamorously dishevelled mane of model on cover bears no resemblance to my awful mop, now going in *toutes directions*. Dismal picnic in car. Return to hotel to find it's only two o'clock – oh bored de la mère. Thank God for two mosquito bites to scratch. Long to read. Instead children and I go for sodden walk on beach. Ashamed at failure to amuse them better, make up soppy story about mermaids using shells to eat out of. Later, owing to dwindling funds, drink three-franc litre bottle of wine in bedroom. Dinner same as yesterday except *Potage Bonne Femme* has acquired some grated carrot and graduated into *Potage Crécy.*

Night's sleep ruptured again by my son in midnight hysterics, convinced he's turning into a mermaid. No one's ever turned into a mermaid, I say. 'How do you know?' he says. 'You don't know everyone in the world.' Then he asks, do I think Daddy is going to divorce me? Say I hope not, without a tremendous amount of conviction. My son says gloomily that you never know with men.

Thursday: Escape through torrential downpour to gift shop in village to buy present for daily woman. Find rest of GB wives engaged in same pursuit, dickering in ringing voices between repulsive crinolined ladies made entirely of shells, and green glass balls in fishing net. Remember one daily woman telling me she had a whole wardrobe of glass balls brought back by various employers; decide to buy scent on ferry instead.

Another grisly picnic. Everyone prickly, perhaps that's why it's called a holly-day. My husband and I decide to go home tomorrow, a day early. Depressed by rapture with which children receive this news. Go back and pack – heaven to have something to do – and drink in our room. Fast becoming litre bugs.

Friday: Glorious hot sunny day for journey – naturally. Refuse to be charmed by rain-washed beauty of Brittany countryside – like a child suddenly behaving well for last fortnight of term, after you've given him a lousy report, it's come good too late. As we have more money than we thought, the plan is to drive to Abbeville for luxurious last night. But we do not stop for lunch until 3.15 and, as my husband hurtles through Normandy like Patton himself, and the signposts for Boulogne start rearing their ugly heads, I slowly come to horrid realisation that he is aiming to make the boat tonight. Proceed to sulk shamefully. However catastrophic holiday has been, not yet adjusted to prospect of going back to London.

'Forty quid saved and home by midnight,' says my husband joyfully, as the car rattles up the ramp. 'Hooray,' shout the children, 'no more rotten picnics.' Only three suitcases of washing, I think sourly.

Land at Folkestone. Every signpost on motorway beckons us towards Maidstone and London. As a result of too much brandy on the boat, and reminder that owing to untimely death of Senior Dog there will be no Maidstone to welcome me when we reach London, sob quietly all the way home.

But as usual my husband is right; the moment we reach dear Putney, even I perk up. 'Well, I didn't have a nice time,' I hear my daughter telling a friend next morning. 'But at least Mummy enjoyed herself and had a lovely rest.'

Heavenly Banana Skins

One truth I have learnt, as middle age enmeshes me like Virginia creeper, is that I shall never change – because my capacity for self-improvement is absolutely nil. I long and long to be thin – new every morning is the diet in fact – but slowly it's dawning on me that I'm far too greedy ever to reach eight stone.

All the papers persuade me that skirts are getting shorter and straighter, requiring slender legs and 35-inch hips. But I still won't persevere with my press-ups for more than a couple of days, or remember to rotate my ankles at idle moments in the Tube. And I've given up pinching my calves every morning in the bath – it's far too painful.

Besides yearning to be thin, I long to be the world's greatest lover, and occasionally launch fervent campaigns to improve myself in bed. The last one was triggered off by reading a piece on a famous courtesan whose vaginal muscles were so powerful that the gynaecologist once got his hand stuck. So I made a vow that instead of panicking about my overdraft when I woke, I would try flexing my internal muscles a hundred times a day.

For a few days it worked; I lay listening to the dawn chorus, flickering away inside like an indicator. Then a particularly vitriolic letter arrived from my bank manager, sending me whimpering back to my money worries.

Oh, I'll never be willowy, I'll never be deft, I'll always be the sort of slut who only remembers to wash her ears every day when she's in love. I used to have fantasies that if we had a big house and a fleet of servants to tidy up after me, I wouldn't be a slut, but it isn't true. A big house just means more rooms to mess up, and if you have minions, you simply become a cupboard slut. The rest of the house is tidy, but chaos festers and boils like compost, in your study, your bedroom drawers and your wardrobe – a ton of washing behind closed doors.

Sometimes I make pathetic attempts to improve my mind – trying to learn the meaning of every word in the dictionary, but I always fall by the wayside after the beginning of the 'A's, which is why I'm so hot on words like 'abiogenesis' and 'abomasum', which while we're on the subject of great truths, means the fourth or *true* stomach of a ruminant. Maybe if I had four stomachs, even *I* might get frightened into trying to reach eight stone.

I've also come to terms, sadly, with the fact that I'm never going to be able to read all the books in the world, but every so often I try to read the whole of Shakespeare or the Bible, putting the book firmly in the loo and pledging to finish a whole Act every time I go in there. But then invariably I get to one of the Henrys' battle scenes first thing in the morning, and it's impossible to concentrate with so many alarums and excursions outside the door, and cries of 'Mumm-ee, where's my recorder?' So Shakespeare gets carried into the bedroom to be finished while I'm dressing, and sinks never to be found again among the flotsam on my dressing table.

But if I can't change myself, I find outside influences can change me. Last year, for example, I voted Tory and sent my son to boarding school – near-fascist behaviour which would have sent a shiver down my spine ten years ago, but which in the light of events seemed the right thing to do. My son appears to be thriving at boarding school. Mrs Thatcher has yet to prove herself.

When I was young, too, I remember thinking what a fuss middle-aged people made about my long telephone calls, and how I wished they wouldn't always fill me up with food when I was trying to diet. I swore I would never be like that. Today, alas, now I am middle-aged, I find nothing drives me to greater irritation than young people waltzing into the house, commandeering the telephone, making calls without asking, or immediately getting a stream of incoming calls. Equally, when I've blued half the housekeeping money on a leg of pork which is sizzling in the oven, because I feel that with 34-inch hips like that the young need feeding up, I find it difficult not to get tight-lipped when they suddenly announce they've gone vegetarian.

Another truth bitterly learnt is that whenever I get slightly pleased with myself, and think I'm doing something rather well, up in heaven God starts peeling a banana skin. The moment, for example, I begin to think of a particular dish as 'one of my specialties' – fish pie, perhaps, or *bœuf en croûte* – and serve it up at dinner parties with a flourish, it starts tasting like old socks. The moment I begin thinking I'm rather attractive, because three men have asked me out to lunch in one week, they all cancel, and it's back to frump again.

I've discovered, too, that crime is invariably followed by punishment. Grovelling round in the dew-soaked undergrowth this morning, trying to divert a clematis back over our garden wall, so that we – rather than our neighbours – might reap the benefit of its purple glory, I snapped it off at the roots. Trying to get out of the grisly rat race of organising non-stop games at my daughter's birthday party, I decide lazily to take all her little friends to the cinema, and find that the only films on are *Midnight Express* and *The World Is Full of Married Men*.

And while on the subject of children, I have learnt that nothing double-glazes a dinner party quicker than two women talking across a table about education, and that more useless worry is wasted on the progress of one's children, whether they are crawling or walking or reading or dating, than anything else. I once planted seven begonias in the conservatory. Within a few days one was putting forth curly green leaves; within a further few days, five others followed suit; only one, planted in a broken green flowerpot, showed no progress at all. It was nearly left for dead. In the end, though, they all grew tall and flowered beautifully. But the one that bloomed most exquisitely and gave pleasure with its lovely white flowers long into the depths of winter was the little late developer.

We want our children to get on because it reflects creditably on ourselves. Which brings me to yet another truth: how much our lives are ruled by vanity, and what a great sexual deterrent it is. I was once sorely tempted to embark on a passionate affair with a distinguished poet, when suddenly he started talking about a beautiful and eminent lady novelist. He had not been able to go to bed with her more than once, he said, because he had felt 'absolutely suffocated, my dear, by her vast, pink, marshmallow thighs'. Well, she was much thinner than me, so I decided not to give him the chance to compare us.

In the same way, a man will often find a girl refusing to come out with him because she fancies him too much to allow him to see her with a cold sore. Or a secretary may refuse to let her boss kiss her for the first time behind the filing cabinets after work because she hasn't cleaned her teeth since breakfast. We all like others to see us in a favourable light, which is probably why the most difficult thing when you begin to live with someone is getting used to going to the lavatory in such close proximity. Perhaps this explains why so many couples get constipated on dirty weekends.

About love I have learnt nothing, except that one learns nothing from experience and that I will always turn into a fishwife if my security is seriously threatened. One of the greatest shocks of my life was that a happy marriage doesn't extinguish desire. About eighteen months after I got married, I went to a party without my husband, and met a publisher with Cambridge-blue eyes, who walked me home and gave me a huge branch of blossom from one of the cherry trees in The Boltons, and I was thrown into a panic of self-hatred because I fancied him so much. Now, after eighteen years, I realise that in turn desires do not extinguish a happy marriage, they only strengthen it because you realise what you've got already is so much better for you. On the other hand, from the cosily insulated security of the married state, it is very easy to forget how much those unhappy in love can suffer, and how lonely people living on their own can be.

I have also found that most couples are far too busy battling to survive financially; that the most unfaithful husbands are always the most insanely jealous if their wives even glance at another man; that if a husband says, 'Oh, old Samantha doesn't like sex very much,' it usually means she doesn't like it with him.

Finally, each year as I get older, life gets better and I get intense pleasure out of my books, my work, listening to music, my garden, my dogs, my friends, my family and my lovely Common rippling green and rain-rinsed down to the river. But I am getting smug again. Far up above I can hear God stretching out to the heavenly cornucopia for another banana.

Middle-aged Wife's Tale

My first piece for the *Sunday Times* appeared thirteen years ago in the colour magazine, before I got a regular column in the paper. Entitled 'The Young Wife's Tale', it described the joys and problems of our first years of marriage.

Since then marriage has been under siege, leaving the stage littered with bodies. Women's Lib has come and not gone. Wives, we are told, are leaving their husbands in droves because of the rawness of their deal. Divorce, a hideous spectre at the wedding feast, stoppeth one in three like the Ancient Mariner.

Watching the three-legged race at my daughter's sports day last year, I was struck by how much the couples symbolised today's two-career marriage. Some stumbled past supporting one another, others fell over and packed it in in a flood of tears, some of the speediest runners were hopelessly impeded by slow partners, yet a few, obviously after a lot of practice, had managed to achieve a smooth and steady progression.

A friend depressed me immeasurably the other day by bitterly quoting Margaret Drabble's claim that one cannot have a career, children and a husband – something has to go, usually the husband. On reflection, I decided this was defeatist and, if you were lucky enough to have the right husband, all three were possible.

People often wonder how Mrs Thatcher got to the top while looking after a husband and two children. I found out at a party at Downing Street earlier this year. Arriving twenty minutes after it was due to start, I found only Denis and a couple from the GLC occupying the huge double drawing room. Mrs Thatcher, explained Denis, had been coping with the miners and would be down soon. I was just thinking how nice he was, and how infinitely less of an ass than his public image suggests, when in swept Mrs T., looking ravishing in dark blue frills, wafting scent from her bath-warm body like regalia lilies at twilight. Instantly Denis turned to her, saying:

'Darling, how lovely to see you, and how marvellous you look.'

There was no question of the pride and delight in his voice, or the affection between them, and I realised what a tremendous support he must have been to her over the years.

Denis is a rarity. 'The majority of husbands,' said Balzac, 'remind me of an orangutan trying to play the violin.' Though not putting myself remotely in the same league as Mrs Thatcher, I, too, am lucky to be married to a rarity, a husband who picks up my every vibe, who senses when I'm getting overtired, and who, realising there are times when writers must write, will calmly take over running the house and looking after the children.

Some things of course have had to go. Twelve years ago, Hunter Davies told me that when he, or his wife, Margaret Forster, were working on a book, they never went out in the evenings. I was appalled. In those days, my life was strung like a paper chain from party to party. Today, there are weeks on end when we hardly go out, seldom entertain, and spend all weekends at home, tidying up the mess I've made during the week, de-jungling the garden, or both simply working. Sadly, one loses friends, but the real ones understand and wait for us to resurface.

In the old days I tried, like Mrs Thatcher, to cook my husband's breakfast, but merely filled the house with the smell of charred toast. Better to marry and not to burn. Now I merely drop a multi-vitamin pill into a glass of water. Sometimes as a treat, I take it up to him in bed. I used to cook a two-course dinner in the evenings during the week, because I wanted to emphasise my cherishingly wifely role. Experience has taught me if I stop work at eight o'clock, he would much prefer an hour's chatter over a couple of drinks, and later baked beans on toast or scrambled egg.

We also turned our dining room into a second drawing room, so we can unwind in peace without being interrupted by double somersaults and shrill voices arguing over the relative merits of television programmes. A dressing room for Leo helped, too, so he could escape from the flotsam of my clutter. Separate cars – albeit two bangers just able to limp through their MOT – also added to our marital harmony. No longer at 8.30 in the morning do I find the car gone, and six little girls frantic to be transported to school. Separate razors also reduced our squabbling dramatically.

But not separate beds. In a two-career marriage, it is all too easy to skip sex when you're both exhausted and under pressure. Only when you have it, do you realise how much you needed it, and what tension was caused by its lack. With my body, I thee worship, says the Prayer Book wisely, which means not only revere but regularly attend. Although, as a girlfriend who dotes on her husband remarked the other day: 'It is rather hard to worship Jamey some mornings, when he wakes up smelling like a sewage farm: cigars, whisky, last night's curry, and the general dyspepsia of middle-aged stress.'

In a marriage as intense as ours, jealousy, too, is inevitable. Even today when I talk to my mother on the telephone for longer than five minutes, Leo starts banging pans, and all the way down the wires from Brighton, I can hear my father irritably rustling *The Times*. I myself get sick with jealousy if I think Leo is interested in someone else. His methods are more direct. The other day, when I'd been talking to a man on the sofa for half an hour with all the absorption of sudden mutual attraction, in walked Leo with a plate of cut-up oranges, which he thrust under our noses, saying: 'Half time.'

With middle age, too, one has less and less inclination to wander. The spring always unsettles me a little, but it's such a hassle after an illicit lunch, rushing home, getting back into my old clothes, washing off my make-up and the scent behind my ears, so I'll look normal when Leo returns from work.

The children grow more watchful, too, and have recently come up with middle stump questions like: 'Have you ever mated with anyone else but Daddy?'

My poor secretary was slightly nonplussed the other day, when (in the car, of course, where there's no direct eye-contact) one of them asked: 'How old were you when you had your first organism?'

At thirteen and ten, I have to confess they have reached most enchanting ages, lovely to talk to, incredibly kind and considerate, and – because they've had to be – very self-sufficient. They can get their own breakfasts, Hoover if need be, go to the shops for me, do the vegetables, and best of all, leave me alone with a hangover in the morning. One friend admitted the secret of her happy marriage was teaching both her children to iron their own clothes from the age of six.

Job's comforters assure me I'm living in halcyon days. You'll never get a wink of sleep, they warn me, once Emily starts going out with boys, and Felix is old enough to drive. I can't wait, he'll be able to drive me all over London and save a fortune in minicab bills.

If Leo and I row over the children, it's principally because he has higher standards than I do, and detests any of us watching rubbish on television. Every week last summer, I, the children, my secretary, three dogs and four cats squeezed in a decadent row on to the sofa, and, in the blazing afternoon sunshine, sat glued to the repeats of *Dallas* (which we hadn't been allowed to watch first time round), praying the 22 bus would get stuck on the bridge and Leo wouldn't get home in time to catch us.

Another reason marriage is under siege at the moment is that most couples have less money than they used to, which makes people very bad-tempered. Two years ago, when we were so seriously in debt that the bank urged us to sell our house, and I spent every day in the potting shed hiding from our creditors, Leo and I absolutely crucified each other. Raw with resentment, we seemed to be fighting every evening. Baked beans lose their charm when they're the only thing you can afford.

Happily things got better, and we both cheered up. As my daughter said to one of her little friends, who'd been bawled out by her workaholic father: 'Why don't you borrow my daddy for a bit, he's got *so* much nicer since he changed his job.'

So many husbands have been forced to become workaholics to make ends meet or because they're terrified of losing their jobs, and as a result neglect their wives. Others have been laid off or got the sack and, macho dented, slink around at home, getting in the way. One has only to listen to the wifely acrimony in the fish queue: 'When I came in from work, he'd done sod all except the junior crossword, and leave splashes all over the sink. Hadn't even washed up the children's breakfast.'

For others cumulative irritation, not lack of money, is the last straw. Two years ago, I met an enchanting girl at the races, only to be told the next day that she'd recently murdered her husband, plunging a carving knife into him because he'd asked her for the hundredth time whether the small forks went inside the big forks.

I've never taken the carving knife to Leo. But one evening during our financial crisis, I walked into the bedroom very proudly wearing a dark brown woollen nightie trimmed with white lace which I'd bought for twopence at a jumble sale, only to be told to take it off at once because I looked like a 'disgusting old friar'. Later that night when he was sleeping peacefully and I heard one of the dogs drinking out of his water mug, I merely laughed and turned over.

Leo is also keen on honesty in marriage, which, because I'm the more hopeless, usually boils down to a vigorous listing of my ineptitudes. Some days he comes home in a picky mood (usually because he's had to wait hours in the cold for the 22 bus) to find all the lights blazing. Having banged around upstairs, he comes into the kitchen demanding *why* I'm opening a tin of cat food, when there are already three gathering mould in the fridge, *why* I persist in putting knives the wrong way up in the washing-up machine and putting crosses in sprouts, which only makes them soggy, and *why* I don't let him do the potatoes because he does them so much quicker.

After a long pause, he asks me why I'm sulking, to which, through gritted teeth, I reply that I am not. Whereupon he points out the muscle going in my cheek, and suggests I must have the curse coming. He then progresses to the vegetable rack, and discovering the rotting spinach dripping dispirit-edly on to the wrinkled carrots, demands why I waste money all the time.

At this point, I usually take the fight into the enemy camp, by pointing out the massive chunk his Wheeler's bill is taking out of our joint account, to be told sharply that we are not talking about *him* and why do I always fight dirty. I then retire and fight dirtier, by cleaning the bath with his flannel.

After twenty years, he has learnt to cater for my chronic disorganisation. What rocks the boat are my occasional attempts at efficiency. As a result, this year we paid the mini-cab bill twice and the electricity bill three times. Leo also got two anonymous valentines, date-stamped by the office, because I couldn't remember whether I'd posted the first one. Thinking I'd plan ahead when his father came to stay last week, I organised the shopping on Friday, telling him on Saturday morning that all we lacked was some olive oil. Naturally he didn't believe me, and we ended up with twenty-four croissants, 6lb of broad beans, 3lb of mushrooms, and two legs of pork.

Partly from a dread of getting into debt, and partly from laziness, I never get anything mended or done to the house. Consequently, Leo is forced to extremes. The other day I had a particularly difficult piece to finish, when an electrician arrived to fix the bathroom light string, which, after months of it being so short we had to climb on to a chair to pull it on with our nails, had finally disappeared. The electrician was followed by a man to measure some carpets, followed by a nice man delivering five massive cabinets to accommodate what is laughingly known as my filing, which completely blocked up the hall. Finally two undergraduates rolled up to remove the eight-foot-high toy cupboard, which Leo had decided was an eyesore on the top landing. Within an hour they had completed the task, leaving me in hysterics, and twelve years' accumulation of overpriced plastic and leaking board games all over the top floor.

Unwisely I telephoned Leo and screamed.

'I told you they were all coming,' he said.

'You didn't, you didn't.'

'I did, but you were, as usual, too wrapped up in yourself to listen.'

The middle stump again.

'Is Daddy going to divalse you?' asked my daughter as I came off the telephone. Leaving me to ponder gloomily who on earth would put up with me if he did. Besides, I like sleeping on the left side of the bed, and who else would do my VAT and tolerate a multi-vitamin pill for breakfast? I would also miss being married to the Escoffier of Putney. We may not bother much during the week, but at the weekend Leo does run up the most delicious food: sea trout with curried prawns, kipper pâté wrapped in bacon *en croûte*. He was once making a spinach tart when the mixer exploded, coating the ceiling with a most attractive veneer of green purée, which remained there for eighteen months until we had the kitchen painted.

Which brings me to weight – not middle-aged spread exactly, since I weigh the same as I did the day I got married, but sadly the world has got thinner. Watching a clip of Real Madrid playing Eintracht Frankfurt in the sixties on television the other night, the players all looked as fat as butter compared with today's lithe demigods. It's bad enough making ends meet financially, but even worse trying to join the ends of one's waistband. The only answer is a nappy pin. The fiercest fights in our house in fact are over the custody of the last nappy pin. To keep the peace, I recently despatched my secretary to buy separate ones.

'Blue or pink?' asked our local chemist, who prides himself on being the fount of all Putney gossip.

'Both,' said my secretary.

'Don't tell me,' said the chemist, falling over the counter in his excitement, 'that Mrs Cooper's expecting twins!'

Over twenty years, though, we are gradually learning tolerance. Marriage – Margaret Drabble again – is a complex game of bargaining. I put up with Leo's ancient incontinent tabby cat, he grits his teeth when the puppy chews up his batting gloves. He was nice when I forgot to pack the sponge-bag recently, I was nice when his bonfire singed my new syringa bush. And if I'm sometimes incensed by his sense of fair play (nothing irritates me more at an international when he stands up and applauds a try scored by the other side), I am touched by his fierce loyalty. In his office drawer, he has a supply of postcards of Beachy Head. On the back of which, he writes, 'Why don't you go and jump off it?' to anyone he considers has been unkind to me.

But perhaps most precious of all in our marriage is the friendship, the sharing of experience, the hysterical private jokes that shake the bed, the post-mortems after parties, the luxury of having someone loving you despite spare tyres and crêpe on the thighs, the living in each other's heart, the haunting fear that one day one of you must die. Will you still need me, will you still feed me when I'm sixty-four?

Flipping through my diaries for the last twelve years, I am shocked by the records of rows and the number of times I have written, 'Leo and I are getting on horribly at the moment.' Yet looking back on our marriage, I only remember the happy times, as one's childhood always seemed filled with sunshine and buttercups.

One in three marriages breaking up is a chilling statistic, bringing appalling unhappiness to adults, and even worse to children. Surely couples should distinguish between a bad patch which may improve, and a total marital breakdown, and try a bit harder. From my diaries, there are half-a-dozen times when I thought of bolting. Thank God I didn't.

Every day when I walk my dogs at lunchtime, I meet a couple who must be in their late seventies, possibly eighties. She is a very pretty woman, and in summer wears a straw hat with yellow flowers. They walk hand in hand, slower than they did eight years ago, but they always seem to be laughing and delighting in each other's company. They have been married fifty years. That to me is achievement, a life work as great as painting the Sistine Chapel.

The pattern of flowers on the outside of my wedding ring is almost worn away, but inside as deep as ever is engraved: L.C. 7.10.61. J.S. I hope, in thirty years, I shall be lucky enough to write a piece to celebrate my golden wedding called 'An *Old* Wive's Tale'.

Acknowledgements

My thanks are due to the editor of the *Sunday Times*, in which these pieces appeared in the first place.

I am also hugely grateful to Transworld for reprinting them, particularly Larry Finlay, Managing Director, Patsy Irwin, Publicity Director, and her terrific publicity team, and to Sally Williamson, the marvellous Senior Commissioning Editor.

I am also blessed with a fantastic agent at Curtis Brown, Felicity Blunt, and her lovely assistant, Rosie Pierce.

It was Sally Williamson and Rosie Pierce who very nobly read through the originals and selected the ones they most enjoyed, to which I added a few of which I was particularly fond.

I would also like to add a special thanks to my PA, Amanda Butler, who is not only the kindest person in England, but who keeps my life running smoothly and ties up the loose ends.

Finally, I am so grateful to my son Felix and my daughter Emily, who, when children, starred in so many of these pieces, and to their lovely families who bring me such joy every day.

RIDERS

Riders, the first and steamiest in the glorious Rutshire chronicles series, takes the lid off international show jumping, a world in which the brave horses are almost human, but the humans frequently behave like animals.

The brooding hero, gypsy Jake Lovell, under whose magic hands the most difficult horse or woman becomes biddable, is driven to the top by his loathing of the beautiful bounder and darling of the show ring, Rupert Campbell-Black. Having filched each other's horses, and fought and fornicated their way around the capitals of Europe, the feud between the two men finally erupts with devastating consequences at the Los Angeles Olympics.

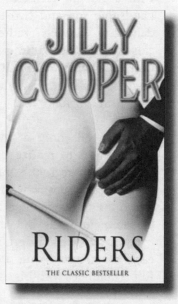

'Sex and horses: who could ask for more?'
Sunday Telegraph

'Blockbusting fiction at its best'
Mail on Sunday

'I defy anyone not to enjoy her book. It is a delight from start to finish'
Daily Mail

RIVALS

Into the cut-throat world of Corinium television comes Declan O'Hara, a mega-star of great glamour and integrity with a radiant feckless wife, a handsome son and two teenage daughters. Living rather too closely across the valley is Rupert Campbell-Black, divorced and as dissolute as ever, and now the Tory Minister for Sport.

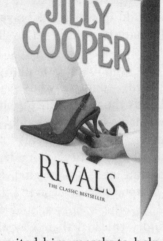

Declan needs only a few days at Corinium to realize that the Managing Director, Lord Bad-dingham, is a crook who has recruited him merely to help retain the franchise. Baddingham has also enticed Cameron Cook, a gorgeous but domineering woman executive, to produce Declan's programme. Declan and Cameron detest each other, provoking a storm of controversy into which Rupert plunges with his usual abandon.

In bed and boardroom, the race is on to capture the Cotswold Crown . . .

'Jilly Cooper is the very best . . . Elegant, glamorous, wonderful fun'
Daily Mail

'A combination of drama, sex and good social comedy . . . Unputdownable'
Sunday Times

POLO

In Jilly Cooper's third Rutshire chronicle we meet Ricky France-Lynch, who is moody, macho, and magnificent. He had a large crumbling estate, a nine-goal polo handicap, and a beautiful wife who was fair game for anyone with a cheque book. He also had the adoration of fourteen-year-old Perdita MacLeod. Perdita couldn't wait to leave her dreary school and become a polo player. The polo set were ritzy, wild, and gloriously promiscuous. Perdita thought she'd get along with them very well.

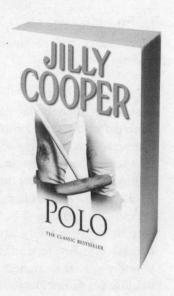

But before she had time to grow up, Ricky's life exploded into tragedy, and Perdita turned into a brat who loved only her horses – and Ricky France-Lynch.

Ricky's obsession to win back his wife, and Perdita's to win both Ricky *and* a place as a top class polo player, take the reader on a wildly exciting journey – to the *estancias* of Argentina, to Palm Beach and Deauville, and on to the royal polo fields of England and the glamorous pitches of California where the most heroic battle of all is destined to be fought – a match that is about far more than just the winning of a huge silver cup . . .

'Compulsively readable and funny . . .
the irrepressible Jilly remains irresistible'
The Times

MOUNT!

In Jilly Cooper's latest, raciest novel, Rupert Campbell-Black takes centre stage in the cut-throat world of flat racing.

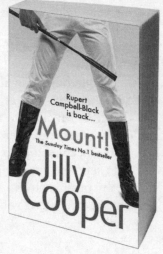

Rupert is consumed by one obsession: that Love Rat, his adored grey horse, be proclaimed champion stallion. He longs to trounce Roberto's Revenge, the stallion owned by his detested rival Cosmo Rannaldini, which means abandoning his racing empire at Penscombe and his darling wife Taggie, and chasing winners in the richest races worldwide, from Dubai to Los Angeles to Melbourne.

Luckily, the fort at home is held by Rupert's assistant Gav, a genius with horses, fancied by every stable lass, but damaged by alcoholism and a vile wife. When Gala, a grieving but ravishing Zimbabwean widow moves to Penscombe as carer for Rupert's wayward father, it is not just Gav who is attracted to her: a returning Rupert finds himself dangerously tempted.

Gala adores horses, and when she switches to working in the yard, her carer's job is taken by a devastatingly handsome South African man who claims to be gay but seems far keener on caring for the angelic Taggie. And as increasingly sinister acts of sabotage strike at Penscombe, the game of musical loose boxes gathers apace . . .

'Packed with warmth, wit and unforgettable characters, this
is an utterly joyous read . . . a complete delight'
Daily Express